Continuing
the
Inquiry

D1114070

"Nothing is possible without men;
nothing is lasting without institutions."

Jean Monnet
Memoirs (1978)

Continuing the Inquiry

The Council on Foreign Relations from 1921 to 1996

Peter Grose

A Council on Foreign Relations Book

JX
27
G76
1996

COUNCIL ON FOREIGN RELATIONS BOOK

The Council on Foreign Relations, Inc., is a nonprofit and nonpartisan organization devoted to promoting improved understanding of international affairs through the free exchange of ideas. The Council takes no institutional position on policy issues and has no affiliation with the U.S. government.

From time to time books, monographs, and reports written by members of the Council's research staff or others are published as a "Council on Foreign Relations Book." Any work bearing that designation is, in the judgment of the Committee on Studies of the Council's Board of Directors, a responsible treatment of a significant international topic. All statements of fact and expression of opinion contained in Council books are, however, the sole responsibility of the authors or signatories.

If you would like more information on Council publications, please write the Council on Foreign Relations, 58 East 68th Street, New York, NY 10021, or call the Publications Office at (212) 734-0400.

Copyright © 1996 by the Council on Foreign Relations®, Inc.
All Rights Reserved.
Printed in the United States of America.

This book may not be reproduced, in whole or in part, in any form (beyond that copying permitted by Sections 107 and 108 of the U.S. Copyright Law and excerpts by reviewers for the public press), without written permission from the publishers. For information, write Publications Office, Council on Foreign Relations, 58 East 68th Street, New York, NY 10021.

Library of Congress Cataloging-in-Publication Data

Gross, Peter, 1934-
    Continuing the inquiry : the Council on Foreign Relations at 75 /
    Peter Grose.
        p.   cm.
    Includes bibliographical references and index.
    ISBN 0-87609-192-3
    1. Council on Foreign Relations—History. 2. United States—
Foreign relations—20th century. I. Title.
JX27.G76   1996
327.75'009'04—dc20
                                                                    96-33523
                                                                    CIP

96   97   98   99   PB   10   9   8   7   6   5   4   3   2   1

Cover Design: Dorothy Wachtenheim

CONTENTS

ACKNOWLEDGMENT

The Council is grateful for William A. Hewitt's generous gift that made possible the publication of this book.

FOREWORD

IT HAPPENS very seldom indeed that novel and sensible ideas spring forth from the never-ending discourse about U.S. foreign policy. But without all the palaver, such ideas would rarely have a chance to breathe. Since 1921, the Council on Foreign Relations has been the privileged and preeminent nongovernmental impresario of America's pageant to find its place in the world.

For 75 years now, Council members have talked and listened to each other and to outsiders. Along the way, they enjoyed catalyzing instants of insight and lucidity. Short of those rare and cherished moments, members had to content themselves with hearing and making the best arguments of the day, such as they were.

In this volume, Peter Grose chronicles many of these high and low points. We asked Peter to wrestle with this history because he knows our institution well as a member, former senior fellow, former executive editor of our esteemed journal, *Foreign Affairs,* and because he is a journalist and historian of note and integrity. The words and thoughts are his. We on the staff labored only to ensure accuracy. Happily, humor survives, as do rich vignettes of Council quirkiness.

Some readers will lament that this fair history shows the Council as far less conspiratorial and dominant than the folklore would have it. The Grose narrative reaches far back to epic dinner meetings where a homogeneous group of members debated the issues of the day only to discover they could not agree on very much. For the last 20 years, with a diverse group of members, the results have been about the same, though lacking the healing power of cigar smoke.

What was special then and now about the Council is that, for the most part, members have holstered their bile when within the walls of the Harold Pratt House. Discussions and arguments at Council meetings and in *Foreign Affairs* generally have proceeded without rancor and without partisan bite. In addition to this precious civility, Council members have shared the conviction that Americans must know about the world and play a leading role in its affairs.

If the Council as a body has stood for anything these 75 years, it has been for American internationalism based on American interests. If the Council has had influence during this period, it has derived from individual members taking the varied and often conflicting fare of Council meetings and publications to a wider American audience. From *Foreign Affairs* articles by W.E.B. DuBois and George F. Kennan to books by Henry A. Kissinger and Stanley Hoffmann, the Council's role has been to find the best minds and leaders, bring them together with other Council members, and provide forum and stage.

Peter Grose recounts these matters well. Council Chairman Peter Peterson, Senior Vice President Alton Frye (who has worked here about one-third of our history), and I commend his efforts to you.

Leslie H. Gelb
President,
Council on Foreign Relations

THE INQUIRY

IT ALL STARTED as an inquiry, indeed, "The Inquiry." To the select few who knew, this was the name of a working fellowship of distinguished scholars, tasked to brief Woodrow Wilson about options for the postwar world once the kaiser and imperial Germany fell to defeat. Through the winter of 1917–18, this academic band gathered discreetly in a hideaway at 155th Street and Broadway in New York City, to assemble the data they thought necessary to make the world safe for democracy.

Historians still differ about how seriously President Wilson, though a former university president, took this exercise. The notion had been pressed upon him by Edward M. House, his trusted aide; in the modern style, House would be called Wilson's national security adviser. But there is no question about how seriously the intellectuals took their unprecedented mission. Modesty was neither a prerequisite nor even a virtue. "We are skimming the cream of the younger and more imaginative scholars," declared Walter Lippmann, the 28-year-old Harvard graduate who recruited the scholars and managed the Inquiry in its formative phase. "What we are on the lookout for is genius—sheer, startling genius, and nothing else will do."

The vision that stirred the Inquiry became the work of the Council on Foreign Relations over the better part of a century: a program of systematic study by groups of knowledgeable specialists of differing ideological inclinations would stimulate a variety of papers and reports to guide the statecraft of policymakers. What began as an intellectual response to a juncture of history grew into an institution that would thrive through all the diplomacy of America's twentieth century. Perpetually renewing its membership and its mission, reaching out beyond an elite circle to help educate the entire public, the Council grew into a model that is now emulated by a host of newer research centers, in the United States and abroad. Their common challenge is to stimulate concerned citizens in their thinking about power and politics among nations.

"It all started as an inquiry. . ." Colonel Edward M. House (left), proto-national security adviser, seen here with President Wilson, circa 1919.

Colonel House set off for Europe shortly before the November 1918 armistice. The Atlantic crossing proceeded with all the speed then available for this first exercise in high-level shuttle diplomacy (and under destroyer escort to guard against lurking German submarines). His mission was to arrange the U.S. presence at the peace conference and, he decided, to establish reliable sources of information about conditions in Europe. The scholars of the Inquiry had relied upon the books, maps, and documents they could locate, principally in the Library of Congress and the Columbia University library; House determined that the president needed, at the least, something more current.

The scholars of the Inquiry helped draw the borders of post–World War I central Europe over tea at the Quai d'Orsay, a more congenial venue than the plenary sessions held in Versailles' Hall of Mirrors, shown above.

When Wilson himself set sail for Paris a month or so later (House had booked the Americans into the Hotel Crillon), his presidential cruiser could accommodate no more than 23 of the Inquiry scholars. Suspicious diplomats of the Department of State saw to it that these amateurs in foreign policy were confined to quarters in the lower decks. Briefing papers in hand from their study groups, the cadre of the Inquiry suddenly found their intellectual confidence challenged by the working diplomacy of the Paris Peace Conference of 1919.

"Now suddenly there was less time for deliberation," wrote Colonel House's aide, Whitney H. Shepardson. "Also, to their surprise, they found themselves assigned to work on multinational committees—not to study

[4]

problems but to come up with practical solutions. They found themselves down from the ivory tower, testing something with their feet that might be either rock or quicksand."

The historical record of the Paris Peace Conference focuses on the meetings of the major powers: Britain, France, Italy, and the United States. To those of the Inquiry, however, and the colleagues they gathered among diplomatic and military officers in Europe, these plenary sessions mattered little. For them the daily teas at the Quai d'Orsay, the bridge games, the breakfast and dinner meetings of experts from a dozen countries gave enduring personal meaning to the peace conference.

In congenial and civilized encounters, they floated ideas in the noncommittal style of an Oxford Common Room; they noted each others' expertise and forged lifelong friendships without regard to age or nationality. In these unrecorded discussions the frontiers of central Europe were redrawn (subject, of course, to their principals' sanction), vast territories were assigned to one or another jurisdiction, and economic arrangements were devised on seemingly rational principles. "It seemed to us that the drafting of peace would be a brisk, amicable, and hugely righteous affair," wrote Harold Nicolson, one of the young Britons in attendance.

This was all too reassuring to let fade once the statesmen had gone home. On May 30, 1919, a little group of diplomats and scholars from Britain and the United States convened at the Hotel Majestic, billet of the British delegation, to discuss how their fellowship could be sustained after the peace. They proposed a permanent Anglo-American Institute of International Affairs, with one branch in London, the other in New York.

As the American peacemakers drifted home over the next months, they found their fellow citizens absorbed in isolationism and prohibition, thoroughly inhospitable to the ideals of the League of Nations and the other stillborn creations of the Versailles Treaty. Intellectual dynamism was exhausted in "the physical and spiritual breakdown" of the veteran scholars from Paris, wrote Shepardson, who left House's staff to become a pioneer of the American branch.

To be sure, loose associations of idealistic Americans already existed. Industrialist Andrew Carnegie had founded his Carnegie Endowment for International Peace in 1910. A group of public-minded citizens established a League of Free Nations early in 1918 to promote the League of Nations on the then-popular lecture circuits. (When the Senate rejected the League of

Elihu Root (second from left) headed the original Council on Foreign Relations and was instrumental in the founding of its successor. He had been secretary of state and received the 1912 Nobel Peace Prize. He is shown here (left to right) with Council President and former U.S. Ambassador to Great Britain John W. Davis, Secretary of War Newton D. Baker, and *Foreign Affairs* Editor Hamilton Fish Armstrong at the 1930 opening of the Council's 65th Street headquarters.

Nations in 1920, the League of Free Nations became the Foreign Policy Association.)

But it was a more discreet club of New York financiers and international lawyers organized in June 1918 that most attracted the attention of the Americans from the Peace Conference. Headed by Elihu Root, the secretary of state under Theodore Roosevelt and a Nobel Peace Prize laureate, this select group called itself the Council on Foreign Relations. It began with 108 members, Shepardson recorded, "high-ranking officers of banking, manufacturing, trading and finance companies, together with many lawyers." Its purpose was to convene dinner meetings, to make contact with distinguished foreign visitors under conditions congenial to future commerce.

Despite growing opposition to Wilson's internationalism, the early Council members supported the League of Nations, but not necessarily on

Wilson's rationale. As Shepardson put it, they "were concerned primarily with the effect that the war and the treaty of peace might have on postwar business." At an early meeting, for instance, several members stressed economic advantages that could flow from the League; others hastened to register on the record the argument that world peace was surely more important than immediate profits. For whatever reasons, by April 1919 the members' interest in the dinner meetings dwindled, and the Council went dormant.

The scholars of the Inquiry, returning from Paris, saw an opportunity. The American Institute of International Affairs envisioned at the Hotel Majestic could provide diplomatic experience, expertise, and high-level contacts but no funds. The men of law and banking, by contrast, could tap untold resources of finance but sorely needed an injection of intellectual substance, dynamism, and contacts—whether to promote business expansion, world peace, or, indeed, both. This was the synergy that produced the modern Council and promoted its unique utility for decades to come: academic and government expertise meeting practical business interests, and, in the process, helping conceptual thinkers to test whether they stood on "rock or quicksand."

Not until February 3, 1921, did the diverse interests and egos of the two groups permit a preliminary encounter. Merger negotiations proceeded for five months. The established members of the Council rented New York office space at 25 West 43rd Street, and they agreed to enlarge the businessmen's club "by selecting and inviting to membership," as Shepardson put it, "a number of carefully chosen individuals."

A fortuitous transatlantic circumstance solved the problem of naming the surviving organization. The British diplomats returning from Paris had made great headway in founding their Royal Institute of International Affairs. Undeterred by isolationism or the inhibitions of the Americans, they had even acquired an elegant London headquarters, the St. James's mansion once owned by William Pitt, known as Chatham House. The American branch foreseen at the Hotel Majestic, by contrast, seemed unable to keep up.

Gradually dawning upon the American veterans of the Inquiry was the realization that, in the mood of post-Wilson America, they could no longer promote the congenial Anglo-American fellowship of the Peace Conference common rooms. A combined membership of the two branches, London and New York, was simply not on. During the merger negotiations, Shepardson noted that membership in the New York branch would have to be "restricted to American citizens, on the grounds that discussions and other meetings, confidential in nature, would be more productive if participants and speakers knew for sure that the others in the room were all Americans."

To Shepardson fell the task of informing the British colleagues of this unfortunate reality. Crossing to London, he recalled thinking that "it might be quite unpleasant to have to say for the first time that the Paris Group of British colleagues could not be members" of the American branch. "The explanation to the British was begun (shall we say?) haltingly. However, instead of the frigid look which had been feared, the faces of the British governing body showed slightly red and very happy. They had reached the same conclusion in reverse, but had not yet found a good way of getting word to the other side of the Atlantic!"

To make the distinction clear, the American academics were relieved to adopt the name of their preexisting institutional partner. On July 29, 1921, a New York certificate of incorporation was prepared and the new Council on Foreign Relations came into being.

BASIC ASSUMPTIONS

THE NEW COUNCIL was conceived, in the words of its incorporating charter, "to afford a continuous conference on international questions affecting the United States." By its first annual report, November 1922, it had assurance of financial support for the startup years and close to 300 "carefully chosen" members, including Root from the old Council, but also new and promising figures like Herbert H. Lehman, W. Averell Harriman, and John Foster Dulles.

The Council was nonpartisan: Democrats as well as Republicans were respected members. The Social Register carried little or no weight, in itself. As at the Century Association, which many Council members called their social club in New York, well-established Jews enjoyed early membership, in an era when Jews were barred from other clubs. A prominent African American candidate would surely have been considered with interest. Not on the agenda, however, was membership for women; the prospect of a woman "qualified" for the Council's fellowship was simply too remote from the experience of the founding members even to be raised.

Among the charter members was prominent diplomat W. Averell Harriman (right), here with John J. McCloy, former American high commissioner in Germany and chairman of the Council's board from 1953–70.

Immediately arising was the matter of privacy and confidentiality. Like the Inquiry, the Council determined not to publish its proceedings. "The Council never takes part in affairs for the general public," declared Walter Mallory, an early Council officer. Yet, even at the start, a little publicity was not to be shunned. The first distinguished foreign speaker invited to the Council attracted enough popular notice to create a stir: Georges Clemenceau, wartime premier of France and a pillar of the Peace Conference. After due deliberation, the Council directors decided to open the meeting to the public. Council member Otto Kahn, an investment banker, rose to the occasion and rented the Metropolitan Opera House, on his own account, for a grand lecture on November 21, 1922. For the rest of Clemenceau's New York visit, the Council coordinated all his appointments, "lest special interest groups or political factions" attempt to use the visitor to promote their own causes. The Council itself, the early charters declared, "has no selfish purposes; it is an organization of interested and informed people, with a patriotic desire to help their national life and the relations with foreign countries."

The Council's founding fathers appreciated that democracy involved

From its inception, the activities of the Council on Foreign Relations were private and confidential. The 1922 New York visit of French statesman Georges Clemenceau (second from right) was an exception to this rule. This pillar of the Versailles conference was publicly feted by the Council in grand style at the Metropolitan Opera House on November 21, 1922. (Note the 29-year-old Hamilton Fish Armstrong at the far left.)

the factor of public opinion, but they were uncertain at first about how such opinion was to be formed and expressed. They established a program of "study groups" and "discussion groups" (the Council made a distinction: the former were serious and scholarly, the latter more casual, to appeal to members who wanted to learn as much as to talk), aimed at producing a written analysis with policy conclusions by a single author. The purpose was seldom a public statement by the group, much less by the Council as a whole. Rather, as the method evolved, the designated author would guide discussions, present tentative analyses to be considered and criticized by fellow experts and peers, and polish and assemble them in writing under

John Foster Dulles.

his sole responsibility. Rarely would the group leaders attempt to negotiate agreement on a consensus that, in most cases, would have had to be compromised into blandness. Lionel Curtis, a leading light in London's Chatham House, had written that "right public opinion was mainly produced by a small number of people in real contact with the facts, who had thought out the issues involved." The leadership of the New York Council concurred.

The other primary instrument toward this end, the first and always most visible of the Council's projects, was an austere quarterly journal launched in September 1922, called *Foreign Affairs*. This represented a novel idea for the time—a serious and nonpartisan forum for articles on world politics, presenting divergent views that thoughtful lay readers, upon reflection, could accept or challenge. The content was to be readable but uncompromising in intellectual expectations.

The elder statesman Elihu Root wrote the first issue's lead article, arguing that, isolationist or not, America had become a world power and desperately needed an informed public. Other authors in the issue included the foreign minister of the new Czechoslovakia, Eduard Benes; the last finance minister of the Hapsburg Empire, Joseph Redlich; and a New York lawyer just back from the Peace Conference, John Foster Dulles.*

To generate interest in the new publication, the editors sent copies to influential figures the world over, hoping thereby to establish a high-level readership and, equally important, to induce such notables to contribute articles for future issues. Thus, a copy found its way to Karl Radek, an ideologist for the new Bolshevik regime of Russia. A grateful Radek returned the journal to the Council, reporting that he had shown it to Lenin himself, who added his little marginal notes to Radek's. (Interestingly enough, the Lenin/Radek annotations came not in the journal's article about conditions in Soviet Russia but in Dulles's essay assessing European economic problems.)

Though aimed at professionals in diplomacy and international relations, *Foreign Affairs* was offered to anyone who wished to subscribe. Given the prevailing skepticism about the public's interest in absorbing such demanding material, the editors hoped for a circulation of 500. As it happened, double that number subscribed for the first issue; by December the paid circulation rose to 2,700, and it reached 5,000 by the next spring. Other Council publications followed: bibliographies on international affairs, rosters and data on foreign governments, and an annual survey, *The United States in World Affairs.* These came in an era when serious scholars of diplomacy across the world, like the members of the Inquiry a few years before, had few other resources for policy research and analysis.

Yet the Council, like its membership, insisted on an American focus, the world seen through American eyes, the implications for American policy. Its various projects avoided "international relations in general," as an early institutional history explained, and concentrated instead on "American relations with other countries." The flagship quarterly, after all, was called *Foreign Affairs,* not *International Affairs,* or some variant thereof. Established and hitting its stride by the election year of 1928, the journal published two statements of American foreign policy that were unabashedly partisan, Republican and Democratic. The Republican author was a former New York congressman serving as undersecretary of the treasury, Ogden L.

---

* Root and Dulles were the first of more than a dozen American secretaries of state—past, present, and future at the time of their writing—to appear as authors over the coming decades in the pages of *Foreign Affairs,* along with many more of their counterparts among the world's foreign ministers.

Mills; writing for the Democrats was the unsuccessful candidate for the vice presidency in 1920, Franklin D. Roosevelt.*

Awkward in the records of the Inquiry had been the absence of a single study or background paper on the subject of Bolshevism. Perhaps this was simply beyond the academic imagination of the times. Not until early 1923 could the Council summon the expertise to mobilize a systematic examination of the Bolshevik regime, finally entrenched after civil war in Russia. The impetus for this first study was Lenin's New Economic Policy, which appeared to open the struggling Bolshevik economy to foreign investment. Half the Council's study group were members drawn from firms that had done business in prerevolutionary Russia, and the discussions about the Soviet future were intense. The concluding report dismissed "hysterical" fears that the revolution would spill outside Russia's borders into central Europe or, worse, that the heady new revolutionaries would ally with nationalistic Muslims in the Middle East to evict European imperialism. The Bolsheviks were on their way to "sanity and sound business practices," the Council study group concluded, but the welcome to foreign concessionaires would likely be short-lived. Thus, the Council experts recommended in March 1923 that American businessmen get into Russia while Lenin's invitation held good, make money on their investments, and then get out as quickly as possible. A few heeded the advice; not for seven decades would a similar opportunity arise.

DISSENSION

LATTER-DAY CRITICS seem to imagine that the Council on Foreign Relations functioned in those days as an elite club, small, content, and confident in comfortable homogeneity. In fact, from the start the elders of the Council found it necessary to contend with opposing views in their otherwise amicable meetings. Diversity of opinion in the pages of *Foreign Affairs* was one thing; conflicting viewpoints in personal encounters, over brandy and cigars, threatened the decorum that the early members sought above all to maintain.

---

* This election year feature was revived in 1988 by the journal's fourth editor, William G. Hyland. The Democratic and Republican authors were historian Arthur Schlesinger, Jr., and Senator Richard G. Lugar of Indiana, who would be a presidential candidate in 1996.

Anger and dissent among members marred the supposed composure within the first year or so. The flashpoint was an invitation to an avowed isolationist to speak at a private dinner meeting. Bankers and members of the original Council protested. Russell C. Leffingwell, a partner of J. P. Morgan's bank, refused to stand at the lectern alongside an isolationist; Paul Warburg of Kuhn Loeb vented outrage that an "uneducable demagogue" should be offered Council hospitality. Academic members, testing the uneasy partnership with their monied colleagues, fought back. Isaiah Bowman, a stalwart of the Inquiry, responded with incredulity: "What has Wall Street to gain by refusing to hear even a demagogue? Certainly if he is a dangerous demagogue we ought all the more to hear him to discover why he is dangerous and just how dangerous he is."

As the Council's seasons mounted, and the society of the 1920s grew informal and undisciplined, the increasing diversity of views was matched by new and different personal styles of rhetoric and behavior, even in civilized company. Henry Stimson, President Taft's secretary of war and later President Hoover's secretary of state, a Council member since the beginning, expressed annoyance at the "cranks and dissidents" whose carping threatened to discomfort other members at Council meetings.

For all their grumbling, the captains of finance among the membership clearly welcomed the intellectual stimulation and diversity, the unique synergy of interests envisioned at the start. They did all right by their Council. Members who were directors of large corporations seized the opportunity to inject the concerns of business into the reflections of scholars. Some 26 firms signed up for a program of corporate financial support. Capital funds accumulated during the heady decade of the 1920s. With an investment acumen that few of the day could match, the Council liquidated the better part of its portfolio the year before the crash of 1929, realizing $300,000 in cash to purchase a permanent home, a five-story townhouse at 45 East 65th Street, abutting the family residence of Franklin D. Roosevelt, who had become the governor of New York.

Supported by a $50,000 grant from the Carnegie Corporation, the Council launched a major initiative in December 1937 to spread its activities and role across the United States, to replicate the New York Council in eight American cities. Local gentlemen of influence would be enlisted to organize systematic discussions in their own communities. These so-called Committees on Foreign Relations would be autonomous and self-govern-

[15]

ing; they were never intended to be a network governed from New York. Walter Mallory, the Council's operating officer, insisted "that the Committees should not be 'action groups' sponsoring particular policies, but should serve only for the enlightenment of the members."

But the Department of State, for one, did not wait long to try using the new Committees on Foreign Relations to build a popular base for Roosevelt, who had become president in 1933, in his foreign policy. The public liaison officer in Washington, Hugh Wilson, diplomatic doyen of the Versailles generation, invited the Council to "send a man here on current questions. This man could talk with the proper people in the State Department, preparing a memorandum on his own which would not be attributed to the Department, and circulated for the confidential information of the men on the selected [Committees'] list. We could arrange that the men on the selected list would not be notified that this was State Department material." The Council's management tactfully let this dubious suggestion drop.

This very dilemma would trouble the Council for years to come. Along with the synergy of academic and business interests, the Council had the difficult task of protecting its independence in analysis and opinion while maintaining useful proximity to friends and colleagues in government. That proximity, essential to informed discussion, always opened the possibility that a Council occasion could be exploited by one or another faction, as foreign policy debates became more fractious than in the agreeable days of the Paris Peace Conference.

Striving to increase its reach, the Council sought to engage leaders of the American labor movement, recognizing labor as a significant and dynamic factor in the world economy. Financiers, professors, and career diplomats who were becoming influential in governing the Council little understood that labor leaders, who had made their careers in the class struggle against capital and management, might not feel at ease amid the shared assumptions and elite perspectives of the Council.

In the interwar decades America's idea of international affairs, such as it was, tended to be Eurocentric, and this was reflected in the topics given greatest attention in the discussion and study groups in New York and in the Committees across the country. Yet the Council made efforts to direct members' attention to other areas of the world.

The first issue of *Foreign Affairs* included an article on the Pacific islands, conquered remnants of the German empire newly turned by the

Professor of Near Eastern history at Harvard and director of the university's Widener Library, Archibald Cary Coolidge was the first editor of *Foreign Affairs*

League of Nations into "mandates" of the victorious powers. "The introduction of the Mandate principle into the Pacific is an experiment which will be watched with interest," *Foreign Affairs* readers were told. "The administration of backward races and undeveloped areas by individual states, in the Pacific as elsewhere, has hitherto not always been as fortunate as could be desired. There is hope that the Mandate principle of collective international supervision may bring better results and may furnish an example for the administration of backward regions which are now under the full sovereignty of separate Powers."

Then, in April 1925, *Foreign Affairs* broke ground on a radical topic that seemed beneath the notice of conventional diplomatic thinking; once presented, moreover, it was for many an intrusion not to be welcomed.

The continent of Africa appeared to the Council on Foreign Relations in its first decades (reflecting American foreign policy in the period) as a factor of empires and colonies, of untapped natural resources, and, though not often addressed, of avenues for social and economic progress among peoples deemed backward or undeveloped. The views of an African Ameri-

A key Council leader, Hamilton Fish Armstrong assumed the editorship of *Foreign Affairs* in 1928 and remained at the helm for nearly half a century.

can sociologist, W.E.B. DuBois, came to the attention of the 32-year-old managing editor of *Foreign Affairs*, Hamilton Fish Armstrong, who made bold to solicit an article for publication. The journal's chief editor, Archibald Cary Coolidge, resident at Harvard, read the ensuing manuscript and seconded his deputy's eagerness to publish it. "Many who object to it," Coolidge wrote Armstrong, "will do so because the thoughts it suggests make them feel uncomfortable, as in my own case."

The article, "Worlds of Color," the first of five that this author would eventually publish in *Foreign Affairs*, remains remarkable half a century later. DuBois had had first-hand experience with the colonies of Africa and portrayed their diverse societies with an intimacy unmatched in the prevailing colonial literature. Moreover, he went on to inject the issue of race into diplomatic calculations; "I seem to see the problem of the twentieth century as the problem of the color line," DuBois wrote in 1925.

> With nearly every great European empire today walks its dark colonial shadow, while over all Europe there stretches the yellow shadow of Asia that lies across

the world. . . . For while the colored people of today are common victims of white culture, there is a vast gulf between the red-black South and the yellow-brown East.

Color hate easily assumes the form of a religion and the laborer becomes the blind executive of the decrees of the masters of the white world; he votes armies and navies for "punitive" expeditions; he sends his sons as soldiers and sailors; he composes the Negro-hating mob, demands Japanese exclusion and lynches untried prisoners. What hope is there that such a mass of dimly thinking and misled men will ever demand universal democracy for all men?

Latin America was a matter of special concern to Council members, but they regretted that their expertise, acquired largely through their business operations, did not generate much public interest in the United States. A 1935 Western Hemisphere study group proposed that the Council publish its findings "as a contrast to the mistaken notions of the average North American." The group, started as a two-year review of the New Deal's Good Neighbor Policy, incurred the ire of members who resented the implication that U.S. firms had not been "good neighbors" before Roosevelt came into office. The Council management bowed to the sentiments; Good Neighbor Policy was nothing more than "one of those happy phrases politicians love to coin," Mallory declared, and he changed the name of the study group. It became "Current Relations with Latin America," bland enough to satisfy the restive members, but also to remove any element to pique the interest of a broader audience.

Many of the Council grew as worried about militarism in Japan as in Europe. In March 1933, Secretary of State Stimson objected that a Japanese diplomat has been invited to speak, expressing his shock "that the Council on Foreign Relations, with its extremely high, though unofficial standing, should lend itself to furthering the subversive effects of such propaganda." Stimson compared academic members seeking to hear divergent points of view "to those men of Athens whom St. Paul described as solely anxious to hear and discuss some new thing." For his part, "the Council existed for a rather more responsible purpose."

Thus recurred the old reservation about the Council's stance of impartiality that Wall Street members had raised a decade earlier and the more academically inclined had resisted. A few months earlier, the tolerance of Council members had been even more angrily challenged when a visiting

Columnist Dorothy Thompson, shown here in 1939 testifying before the Senate Foreign Relations Committee, was among the first to "dissect the looming Nazi phenomenon" in the pages of *Foreign Affairs*.

German journalist had explained why an upstart politician named Adolf Hitler might have an appeal to many Germans in the years to come. Mallory, ever seeking to calm unrest among the membership, apologized for the controversial speaker's heavy German accent, adding lamely that perhaps he did not understand many of the questions put to him.

Before long, and on a level much more profound than the propriety of divergent views at meetings of the Council on Foreign Relations, a chasm opened within the halls—and across the whole of America.

Armstrong, who had succeeded to the top editorship of *Foreign Affairs* in 1928, was one of the first Americans to interview this man Hitler face to face, in April 1933, less than a month after the Nazi leader assumed dictatorial power in Germany. The young editor emerged from the Berlin chancellery deeply shocked at the values and goals conveyed to him with a demagoguery that the world at large would eventually come to know all too well. He opened his journal to authors who could dissect the looming Nazi phenomenon with more pointed expertise than his own: liberal columnist

Dorothy Thompson; the American socialist Norman Thomas, who denounced Nazi policy toward labor; and historian Charles A. Beard, who attacked Nazi education policies.

During the 1930s, Armstrong began assuming leadership of the Council beyond the pages of his journal. Neither financier nor academic, he used the fresh approach of scholarly journalism to bridge the professional divide. Starting with a question of American law that he judged members would confront more readily than the changing ideologies of a foreign government, he encouraged formation in 1934 of a multiyear study group to examine the U.S. policy of neutrality in the face of fascist aggression. To chair the group, Armstrong promoted an old college friend from Princeton, Allen Dulles, a career diplomat turned Wall Street lawyer who had gained some prominence as an expert on disarmament and collective security.*

Armstrong and Dulles collaborated on a dry but polemical book, published in 1936 under the Council's imprimatur, entitled *Can We Be Neutral?* They attacked the notion, eagerly embraced by isolationist America, that the New World could continue isolating itself from power struggles in Europe and Asia. Interventionist broadsides resounded from *Foreign Affairs* like drumbeats to rouse an apathetic populace. Armstrong prodded another old friend from the Paris Peace Conference, Walter Lippmann, into heights of rhetoric to denounce the Neutrality Act of 1937. "Though collaboration with Britain and her allies is difficult and often irritating," Lippmann wrote, "we shall protect the connection because in no other way can we fulfill our destiny."†

The clash between "interventionists" and "isolationists"—those who agitated to resist totalitarian aggression and those who sought to keep America aloof from foreign power struggles—tore the American intellectual community apart in the late 1930s, as fascism spread across central Europe and the far side of the Pacific. Old friendships among those who had earlier been socially and intellectually like-minded dissolved in anger. Within the

---

* Allen Dulles had actually met Hitler in Berlin two weeks before Armstrong, but as a cautious diplomat he had not allowed himself the passionate reaction of his journalistic friend—a lapse that, under Armstrong's influence, he quickly repaired.

† As it happened, this was the last time the distinguished columnist, an early manager of the Inquiry, would be invited into the pages of *Foreign Affairs*. At the height of the neutrality controversy, Armstrong discovered that his wife and his valued author had fallen into an affair; the two couples were divorced in an unpleasant society scandal. Lippmann and Armstrong's former wife, Helen, subsequently married; the offended editor barred Lippmann from his journal for the rest of their lives.

shelter of the Council and its related advocacy groups, the issue became literally a matter of brother against brother. John Foster Dulles and Allen Dulles, both prominent members respected among their legal and academic colleagues, found themselves on opposing sides. Allen led the cause of intervention to defeat fascism, John Foster argued reasons why the dictators should be appeased.

The schism came to a sudden end only on December 7, 1941, shortly after noon in New York.

WAR AND PEACE

MORE THAN TWO YEARS before the Japanese attack on Pearl Harbor, the research staff of the Council on Foreign Relations had started to envision a venture that would dominate the life of the institution for the demanding years ahead. With the memory of the Inquiry in focus, they conceived a role for the Council in the formulation of national policy.

On September 12, 1939, as Nazi Germany invaded Poland, Armstrong and Mallory entrained to Washington to meet with Assistant Secretary of State George S. Messersmith. At that time the Department of State could command few resources for study, research, policy planning, and initiative; on such matters, the career diplomats on the eve of World War II were scarcely better off than had been their predecessors when America entered World War I. The men from the Council proposed a discreet venture reminiscent of the Inquiry: a program of independent analysis and study that would guide American foreign policy in the coming years of war and the challenging new world that would emerge after.

The project became known as the War and Peace Studies. "The matter is strictly confidential," wrote Bowman, "because the whole plan would be 'ditched' if it became generally known that the State Department is working in collaboration with any outside group." The Rockefeller Foundation agreed to fund the project, reluctantly at first, but, once convinced of its relevance, with nearly $350,000.

Over the coming five years, almost 100 men participated in the War and Peace Studies, divided into four functional topic groups: economic and financial, security and armaments, territorial, and political. These groups met more than 250 times, usually in New York, over dinner and late into the night. They produced 682 memoranda for the State Department, which marked them classified and circulated them among the appropriate government departments.

The European war was only six months along when the economic and financial group produced a lengthy memo, "The Impact of War upon the Foreign Trade of the United States." This was followed by a contingency blueprint in case the British Isles fell to German occupation; Churchill and his ministers would relocate to Canada, the Council analysts concluded, where Anglo-American cooperation in trade would only intensify. In April 1940 and for nine months following, with American entry into the war still only hypothetical, the study group proposed a more tolerant stance toward

As the world edged yet again toward war, Armstrong enlisted his Princeton friend Allen Dulles (shown here at the right with the shah of Iran and Council Director and J. P. Morgan partner Russell C. Leffingwell) to examine U.S. neutrality in the face of fascist aggression.

Japan, hoping thereby to contain Tokyo's expansionist designs on the Pacific islands and the Asian mainland.

The views of the Council group on security and armaments provoked less interest in Washington. Shortly before Pearl Harbor, the group, led by Allen Dulles, outlined the possible need for an American occupation force in defeated Germany, a project that attracted little attention. The territorial group, chaired by Bowman, debated the status of Chiang Kai-shek's China, relative to Japan and the Soviet Union. After a Japanese defeat, the group concluded, China could be opened to American exports and the United States would have access to the raw materials of a vast virgin territory.

Bowman's territorial group registered the one immediate impact of the

President Truman (center) at the Harold Pratt House accompanied by John J. McCloy (at right).

War and Peace Studies upon evolving foreign policy. On March 17, 1940, the Council submitted a memo, "The Strategic Importance of Greenland," advising that, since the Danish outland was properly a part of the Western Hemisphere, it should be covered by the Monroe Doctrine. President Roosevelt promptly invited Bowman for a discussion at the White House, and one day after Nazi Germany occupied Denmark in April, Roosevelt declared American policy along the lines proposed by the Council group, including the intent to establish military bases in Greenland.

The work of the fourth, political, group was largely superseded by the State Department's own postwar policy planning staffs. Nonetheless, the Council group's members were active in the 1944 Dumbarton Oaks conference on world economic arrangements and in the preparations for the 1945 San Francisco conference to establish the United Nations.

Once the United States entered the war, most of the guiding spirits of the War and Peace Studies accepted mobilization into government service, in uniform, in the State Department, or in the fledgling intelligence agency, the Office of Strategic Services. Allen Dulles, for instance, became a pivotal figure in the OSS from a clandestine base in neutral Switzerland, where he had an influential role in implementing the idea he had presented to the Council for an American occupation force in defeated Germany. His brother, John Foster, remained at his New York law firm, Sullivan and Cromwell, throughout the war, but he was active in assisting State Department planning for the future United Nations.

The overall record of the Council's War and Peace Studies can only compare favorably with the performance of its conceptual predecessor, the Inquiry of World War I. Yet its practical contribution to the U.S. war effort, and the political planning for the era following, remains unclear in the judgment of history.

A perennial problem for historians of government is tracing the initiative for any particular political decision within a government, to say nothing of the more tangential outside influences. Clearly, the Council's War and Peace Studies were not as important as Armstrong, for one, chose to regard them in his own retrospect. Yet even the most myopic of diplomatic officials would have difficulty sustaining the argument that American foreign policy could have evolved as effectively without the independent provocation of knowledgeable outsiders. William P. Bundy, who straddled the two worlds in the postwar era, as a Pentagon and State Department official and later as Armstrong's successor at *Foreign Affairs*, concluded, "It has been wisely said that no contingency plans are ever adopted as written, but that the exercise is often invaluable in flagging the questions that must be faced. So it was for this extraordinary exercise, I am sure." [1]

Such were the effects of the upheavals of war upon the habits of society. The primary function of the Council on Foreign Relations during World War II proceeded in rigid secrecy, remote from the slightest awareness of most of the Council's 663 members, who were not themselves personally involved.

THE FIRST TRANSFORMATION

AT WAR'S END the Council stood, like the nation, at a defining moment. Council officers and members, having served the war effort in and out of uniform, filtered back to their private and public lives. Like the generation of their fathers, returning home from Paris, they were eager to sustain the motivation and energy of wartime for the tasks ahead.

Who, actually, was the Council on Foreign Relations at this point in history? An analysis of the officers and directors through the Council's first quarter-century, ending in 1946, revealed both the elitism of the fellowship and the openness of that New York-based elite to new voices, wherever they might be heard.[2] More than half of the Council's leadership during these formative years (35 officers and directors out of 55) had attended Ivy League universities: Harvard, 12; Columbia, 9; Yale, 7. But once graduate schools were added, no fewer than 76 institutions of higher learning were represented. Seven of this leadership group had attended foreign universities; three had studied at Oxford.

Lawyers from the Wall Street firms predominated in the occupational grouping; the 55 Council officers and directors also held 74 corporate directorships. Next came professional academics, with five university presidents, including Bowman of Johns Hopkins and Harold W. Dodds of Princeton. Twelve of the leadership had served in cabinet or subcabinet positions for different administrations in the interwar and wartime years; another 30 had experience elsewhere in the federal bureaucracy, including 21 in the State Department. A typical Council officer belonged to three social clubs from a list of 170; the Century and Knickerbocker in New York and the Cosmos and Metropolitan in Washington were the most popular. The permanent staff of the Council had grown to 20 full-time researchers; the Committees across the country had expanded to 25 from the original 8.

The Council's home on East 65th Street, so grand when acquired after the Wall Street crash, was proving hopelessly inadequate for these expansions. In 1944 the widow of Harold Irving Pratt, a director of Standard Oil of New Jersey and a faithful Council member since 1923, donated the family's four-story mansion, at the southwest corner of 68th Street and Park Avenue, for the Council's use. (In keeping with a prevailing reverse snobbery, the address and front door were on the side street, not the more showy avenue.) John D. Rockefeller, Jr., led a slate of 200 members and companies who volunteered funds to convert the gracious residence into offices, meeting rooms, and an institutional library. When the Council moved into its new quarters in April 1945, Secretary of State Edward Stettinius, a member since 1938, came to New York, "to bear witness [he said], as every Secretary

In 1944 the widow of Harold Irving Pratt, Council member and director of Standard Oil of New Jersey, donated the family home at 68th Street and Park Avenue for the Council's use. "In keeping with a prevailing reverse snobbery, the address and front door were on the side street, not the more showy avenue."

[28]

of State during the past quarter of a century, to the great services and influence of this organization in spreading knowledge and understanding of the
issues of United States foreign policy."*

Intermingled with the meeting and working spaces of the Harold Pratt
House were the editorial offices of *Foreign Affairs*—its circulation by then
grown to 17,000—and an impressive series of periodic reference works for
public use, including *The United States in World Affairs*, a *Foreign Affairs
Bibliography*, and the annual *Political Handbook of the World.*

The budget for this enterprise was transformed of necessity in line with
its staff and operations. Individual bequests from members had provided
some $250,000 for the years following World War II; yet by 1952 the Coun-
cil reported an operating deficit of about $50,000. Over the course of the
1950s large foundations stepped in to support and enlarge the Council as a
leading force in America's international awareness; from the Rockefeller
Foundation and Carnegie Corporation came $500,000 each, topped by $1.5
million from the new Ford Foundation in 1954. The Council had come a
long way from the mellow dinner meetings of the founding years.

In its substance, American foreign policy was similarly transformed in
the first years following World War II. An isolationist frontier nation
became a world power. A wartime ally, the Soviet Union, became an adver-
sary; former enemies, Germany and Japan, became allies. The transformation did not occur without intellectual and organizational agonies—in the
government and in the private associations like the Council that sought to
understand and explain the changes taking place in the world.

Allen Dulles returned from the wartime OSS to assume a leading role in
the Council's business, resuming his law practice at Sullivan and Cromwell
for an interim between his secret work in Switzerland and a career at the
soon-to-be Central Intelligence Agency. Dulles was a Republican; working
alongside him in the Council was Alger Hiss, a newly elected member sym-
pathetic to the left wing of the Democratic Party, but a protégé of the older
Dulles brother, John Foster. Political differences were matched by the egos
and vanities contained within the new Harold Pratt House. Armstrong,
firmly at the Council's helm, grew uneasy that Chatham House, the Council's

---

* Over the coming five decades, the Council acquired and expanded into four adjoining town
houses; by the mid-1990s one-third of the block between Park and Madison Avenues was integrated
into a working headquarters behind the classic facades along a tree-lined New York cross-street.

British counterpart under the charismatic influence of Arnold Toynbee, might seize the initiative in shaping the record of World War II. Armstrong and his colleagues tapped one of their own to compose a comprehensive history of the war: Harvard historian William L. Langer, a scholar involved in the Council since 1932. A historian equally distinguished, Charles A. Beard, promptly denounced the Council and the Rockefeller Foundation for collaborating with the State Department to create a "historical monopoly." These august bodies, Beard declared, did not want "journalists or any other persons to question too closely or criticize too freely the official propaganda and official statements relative to our basic aims and activities during World War II." Beard argued from the left; from the right came columnist George Sokolsky, who described the Council as "a stuffed shirt affair of highbrow internationalists" engaging in "monopolistic scholarship, the sort of thing Hitler did and Stalin does." The dispute turned personal. A Council officer chided Beard for accepting foundation grants—thus dirtying his own hands, if that's the way he chose to look at it, with subsidized scholarship.

Though the Council managed to publish only two volumes of the Langer study, co-authored with S. Everett Gleason, this major work dealing with the period 1939–41 belied Beard's forebodings that supposedly independent scrutiny would only enshrine the official version of the events leading to war. On the contrary, Langer's access to government archives and the two authors' sophisticated analysis produced a new historical record both richer and more nuanced than the policy declarations of the period had envisaged for public consumption.

As the War and Peace Studies came to their end in 1945, the Council reverted to its traditional program for members and the broader constituencies that could be reached through the members' stature and public contacts. In characteristic fashion, Council planners conceived a study group to analyze the coming world order. Notably uncharacteristic was the additional suggestion that the American members be joined by competent persons from Soviet Russia—a joint Soviet-American inquiry. In the congenial, gentlemanly atmosphere of the Harold Pratt House, ideas and visions could be shared.

Percy Bidwell, director of the Council's new Studies Program, had courteously approached the Soviet Embassy as early as January 1944 to stimulate interest in the joint project. He was received by Ambassador Andrei Gromyko, whose response would become all too familiar in the years to come. Through Gromyko the Russian word "nyet" entered the English language. Without any pretense of diplomatic tact, the ambassador (soon to be foreign minister) told the men from the Council he would not permit any responsible Soviet spokesman to join in such a discussion.

Once the truncated inquiry got underway, cold water was thrown in from the opposite side of the ideological spectrum. Historian David Dallin of Columbia, an outspoken figure among anti-Soviet Russian émigrés, took umbrage at the view a left-wing journalist expressed in an early group meeting, that postwar cooperation might be possible with the Soviet regime. "I know from experience that a fruitful discussion of serious problems with a fellow traveler is impossible," Dallin declared. Such thinking was "on such a low level . . . as to make it impossible for me to take part in a meeting at which this gentleman would be present."*

The chairman of the study group, Lazard Frères partner William H. Schubart, a veteran of the War and Peace Studies, pressed on. "I think we can be hard-boiled and just, without doing harm," he told the Council. "The main thing is to be sure that we are not asking for something unreasonable" of the Soviet Union. Specifically, he was pressing for endorsement of a $6 billion loan from the United States to finance Soviet imports for postwar reconstruction. "It seems reasonable to suppose that if economic and political cooperation between Russia and the United States could be developed in peace as military cooperation between the two nations has been developed in war," Schubart said, "the world might look forward to an era of relative stability and considerable prosperity." Bidwell, speaking for the Council's academic staff, concurred. "It seems to me increasingly important that we should be able to break down the intellectual blockade with which the Russians have surrounded themselves."

All the ambiguities that colored American thinking toward the Soviet Union in the first postwar year were embodied in the Council's study group that winter of 1945–46. For enlightenment about Soviet realities, members could only fall back upon secondhand impressions of journalists and scholars, who in turn were analyzing secondhand data many years out of date. As for policy guidance from Washington, none came. A German historian concluded 40 years later, "Suggestions for a future American policy toward

---

* Over the coming years, Dallin went on to denounce the Central Intelligence Agency for attempting to organize anti-Soviet émigrés against the Kremlin, after the new intelligence agency failed to give sufficient attention to his own faction.

the Soviet Union were hardly advanced by these deliberations; rather, the meetings turned out to be merely a process of synchronizing the 'correct' view of the U.S.S.R. among Council members."[3]

It fell to the rapporteur of the study group to try making some sense of the discussions. This unlucky soul was a promising young man named George S. Franklin, Jr., a college roommate of another up-and-coming Council member, David Rockefeller, both of them just beginning long and distinguished careers at the Council. Franklin's task was to assemble perspectives from sources as far apart as Gromyko and Dallin, Lazard's investment bankers and the anti-communists—indeed, in the broader Council, as different as the Dulles brothers and Alger Hiss. For the four months it took him to draft his report, Franklin did his best.

The United States should not disregard the differences between the two nations but should, nevertheless, develop an understanding of the Soviet position and should attempt to work closely with it.

Cooperation between the United States and the Soviet Union is as essential as almost anything in the world today, and unless and until it becomes entirely evident that the U.S.S.R. is not interested in achieving cooperation, we must redouble, not abandon, our efforts, when the task proves difficult. Cooperation, however, does not mean that we should knuckle under, or allow ourselves to become weak. We must bend every effort to make this country strong, prosperous and happy, to relieve cyclical unemployment, and to show the world a way of life that people everywhere will wish to emulate.

The United States must be powerful not only politically and economically, but also militarily. We cannot afford to dissipate our military strength unless Russia is willing concurrently to decrease hers. On this we lay great emphasis.

We must take every opportunity to work with the Soviets now, when their power is still far inferior to ours, and hope that we can establish our cooperation on a firmer basis for the not so distant future when they will have completed their reconstruction and greatly increased their strength. . . . The policy we advocate is one of firmness coupled with moderation and patience.

The Franklin draft was circulated to the study group members early in the spring of 1946. In March, Winston Churchill had delivered his ominous speech about an "iron curtain" descending across central Europe. On May 21, Council members met at the Harold Pratt House to consider the out-

"It's the same thing without mechanical problems."

"It's the 'Internationale.' If you don't know the words, just mumble."

come of their first collective exercise in shaping the postwar world. The heavyweights were in attendance, their swords unsheathed. The 36 members of the study group had tentatively voted on the question of publishing the Franklin draft; 16 seemed inclined to accept it, 5 were likely to vote against, and 15 could not yet make up their minds. (Allen Dulles was one of the Council leaders who remained undecided.)

Leading the charge against the Franklin draft at the plenary was the secretary of the Council's board of directors, Frank Altschul. Though a colleague of Schubart in the investment community, he allowed for no benefit of doubt or deal. The time for negotiation and compromise with Soviet

Russia was over, Altschul declared, and the Council's eager rapporteur was bending over backward to accommodate the Soviet Union.

Once the Wall Street members, with their stature and money, had weighed in so firmly, even the intellectual contingent, Franklin's main mentors at the Council, ran for cover. Bowman, elder statesman of the Council's academics, naturally chose the intellectual plane for his retort. His judgment, nonetheless, was devastating. The draft report was outdated, he informed Franklin. Even worse, it represented mostly "ordinary off-the-cuff opinion that does not represent fresh analysis or thought. . . . A report on so important a theme for so many meetings of a substantial group of men will be taken as the measure of the work of the Council on Foreign Relations. . . . Neither scholars nor policymakers in Washington will consider this report as either excellent or useful."

The Franklin report of May 1946, outlining cautious hopes for cooperative relations between the United States and the Soviet Union in the coming post–World War II years, was dead. The board's committee on studies formally decided against publication in July; by November all sympathy for a conciliatory stance toward Moscow had disappeared from the corridors of the Harold Pratt House. The Franklin draft survives today only in the Council's archives. "It is quite possible," wrote the German historian Michael Wala, "that the Council thus missed an opportunity to give guidance to American policymakers through constructive advice."[4]

"X" LEADS THE WAY

OVER THE NEXT WINTER, an aspiring but weary American Foreign Service officer spent a sabbatical year at the National War College, recovering from his tours of duty in the Baltic states when they were first independent, in prewar Germany, and finally in Stalin's Moscow. George Kennan was irrepressible in his thinking, gifted with the grace of a writer, and troubled by the dilemmas of his conflicting ideas. Through December, he later recalled, he sat "hacking away at my typewriter there in the northwest corner of the War College building."[5]

Kennan shared his intellectual concerns with a small Council study group in January 1947. Among the participants was George Franklin, who rushed to brief Hamilton Fish Armstrong the next morning about the discussion. Armstrong, ever alert to talent and a good article, promptly invited

From the pages of *Foreign Affairs*, George F. Kennan (left) introduced "containment" into the American strategic lexicon. As a young policymaker/diplomat, and (seated in photograph below, left)—no longer anonymous—celebrating his ninetieth birthday with U.S. Representative to the United Nations Madeleine K. Albright and other Council friends at the Harold Pratt House.

the little-known diplomat to adapt his presentation for the Council's journal. Kennan was diffident; he doubted that he, as a government employee, could contribute "anything of value" under his own name. Armstrong persisted, Kennan succumbed. An article, "The Sources of Soviet Conduct," appeared in the July 1947 issue of *Foreign Affairs*. The author was identified only as "X."

Perhaps no single essay of the twentieth century can match the X article for its impact upon the intellectual curiosity of a confused nation, upon the mindset of equally confused policymakers and scholars, upon national policy in at least seven presidential administrations to come.* It ran only 17 pages; its tone was scholarly, elegant but practical; only three sentences used the magic word that came to define American policy for half a century.

"Containment" entered the political lexicon. Walter Lippmann, at the height of his influence as a nationally respected commentator, devoted no fewer than 13 consecutive newspaper columns to a dissection of X's thinking. "Thirteen essays in criticism of one magazine article by a not very anonymous career man in the State Department seems a little out of proportion," wrote Council director Leffingwell to a friend. "Well, Walter gave Ham's magazine some very valuable free publicity."

Kennan's anonymity as X did not survive long, and for the rest of his illustrious career, as an ambassador and intellectual conscience to diplomats and scholars alike, he tried to explain away the "serious deficiencies . . . the misunderstanding almost tragic in its dimensions" that followed from the notion of "containing" Soviet communism. "I should have explained that I didn't suspect [the Russians] of any desire to launch an attack on us," Kennan told an American television audience nearly 40 years later. "This was right after the war, and it was absurd to suppose that they were going to turn around and attack the United States. I didn't think I needed to explain that, but I obviously should have done it."

At the time of its publication, no modifications were forthcoming from the halls of government. What X wrote, and the way it was commonly

---

* Even as this history is being written, I can certify the power of X's rhetoric and vision among students in the 1990s at a major American university. Wary of the first assignment at a supposedly forward-looking seminar—some old article published 30 years before they were even born—and with only the vaguest awareness of the problems the dog-eared text explored, my undergraduates at Yale came back the next week to pronounce the X article "awesome."

interpreted, fit naturally with the foreign policy developing within the Truman administration. The same month as X's publication, Secretary of State George C. Marshall delivered the commencement address at Harvard. He proposed an unprecedented engagement of the United States in the growth and organization of democratic society in Europe. The so-called Marshall Plan and the ensuing North Atlantic Treaty Organization (NATO) defined the role of the United States in world politics for the rest of the century.

Historians and officers of the Council on Foreign Relations are properly reticent about claiming institutional credit for the genesis of the Marshall Plan, despite all the institution's record of interest in economic affairs. "I do not believe that anything organized by the Council played any significant role in framing the Plan itself," wrote William Bundy, although he went on to credit Council study groups with "at least general contributions to the framework of thinking that underlay the Marshall Plan and NATO."

Once out of the starting gate, however, containment, the Marshall Plan, and American commitment to the economic recovery and democratic institutions of Europe became the Council's new interest. Armstrong convened a study group in December 1947 to analyze the political conditions that would make the program of American economic aid most effective. High on the list of worries was the forthcoming election in Italy, where the Communist Party stood a good chance of winning. Council members discussed whether the United States could "give the Italians something"—a battleship or colony or something, as John Sloan Dickey, president of Dartmouth, put it in the sardonic shorthand of experts in after-dinner conversation.

The campaign of public lobbying for this new American outreach was stimulated by countless discussions at the Harold Pratt House, though given the longstanding concern for institutional nonpartisanship on policy the Council would not permit its name to be invoked. Council Director Allen Dulles went so far as to write a full-fledged book arguing for the Marshall Plan, but by the time he completed the manuscript, the cause had already been won; it was published only in 1993, as a footnote to history.

The Council on Foreign Relations functioned at the core of the public institution-building of the early Cold War, but only behind the scenes. As a forum providing intellectual stimulation and energy, it enabled well-placed members to convey cutting-edge thinking to the public—but without portraying the Council as the font from which the ideas rose. Newly named to the post of undersecretary of state in May 1947, Robert A. Lovett, who had first become a member 20 years before, asked for a briefing from Council members and staff before assuming his diplomatic responsibilities. The membership grew toward 1,000, as foreign policy became a public interest far more compelling than the founding luminaries ever imagined.

And, living up to its early promise, *Foreign Affairs* emerged as the authoritative medium for foreign policy discussions by Americans and distinguished foreign leaders, years before television and the Internet allowed for direct communication between statesmen and the public. The roster of Armstrong's authors was impressive by any measure: Adenauer, Erhard, and Brandt of Germany; Mollet of France; Gaitskell, Eden, and Attlee of Britain; Khrushchev of the Soviet Union; Tito of Yugoslavia; Gomulka of Poland; Nasser of Egypt; Dayan of Israel; Spaak of Belgium and the emerging European Community; Magsaysay of the Philippines; Nkrumah of Ghana; Senghor of Senegal; Houphouet-Boigny of the Ivory Coast; Sihanouk of Cambodia. Circulation grew to over 50,000 around the world. A $200,000 donation from Frank Altschul in 1958 underwrote the first expansion of the Council's 68th Street headquarters into the adjoining townhouse, which became the publishing and editorial offices of Council publications.

The temporarily retired General Dwight D. Eisenhower, serving a brief tour as president of Columbia University, agreed to chair a Council study group to monitor the European aid program. He rarely missed a scheduled meeting, until December 1950, when President Truman called him back on active duty to become the supreme allied commander in Europe. "Whatever General Eisenhower knows about economics," said one member later, "he has learned at the study group meetings." Another Council supporter went further to assert that the group "served as a sort of education in foreign affairs for the future president of the United States"—somewhat excessive, perhaps, about an army general who had been deeply engaged with the Allied governments throughout World War II.[6] At the least it can be fairly said that the Council meetings gave a career officer a firsthand (and not always pleasant) taste of the free-wheeling and unstructured manners that civilians use in policy discourse.

Europe dominated the foreign policy agenda until the outbreak of war in Korea in 1950 and, to a large extent, thereafter as well. The Council had little of note to contribute to the domestic debate about the fall of China to communism. Southeast Asia, however, had attracted the Council's attentions starting with the War and Peace Studies. Indochina was seen as a French colonial problem; the consensus of the wartime studies was that France could never expect to return to its Southeast Asian colonies in force, and the region would necessarily become a geopolitical concern of the United States as the emerging Pacific power. After the Korean War ended in 1953, the Council returned to a serious examination of Indochina, where France's restored colonial regime was clashing with the guerrilla forces of a self-described Marxist revolutionary named Ho Chi Minh, whom members of the Inquiry had first encountered as one of the obscure nationality plaintiffs at the Paris Peace Conference more than three decades earlier.

On November 24 a study group heard a political science report from its secretary, William Henderson, more prescient than any of the members could then appreciate. The war was "far larger than anything" the policy thinkers supposed, the group was told. It was wrong to see Ho's Vietminh forces as simply a forward guard of world communism; nothing in Moscow's designs could explain the size and violence of the Vietnamese rebels. Marxism "has little to do with the current revolution"; rather, it was pent-up nationalism, pure and simple. With France discredited by its colonial past, the opportunity was opening for the United States to guide Ho's revolutionaries away from their irrelevant Marxist rhetoric.

Study group members were skeptical, and subsequent speakers from the State Department were far more reserved about discussing any direct American presence in Indochina to fill the political vacuum left by the besieged French. After the final French defeat at Dien Bien Phu in 1954 and for the decade following, the Council's Studies Program often reexamined the unfamiliar spectrum of politics in remote Vietnam. But nowhere in the archives for these years is there evidence that the Council had considered inviting an obscure Vietnamese exile, then living just up the Hudson River from New York, named Ngo Dinh Diem. Diem became the American-sponsored president of South Vietnam in 1956, facing a ruinous civil war before his overthrow and execution in 1963.

Concerns that seemed more pressing bore down at the turn of the 1950s. The nation was in danger of succumbing to a red-baiting frenzy, marked by the rise into the headlines of Senator Joseph R. McCarthy. Not surprisingly, the Council's membership seemed solidly united in contempt for the Wisconsin demagogue; under his provocative rhetoric, after all, was a thinly veiled attack on the entire East Coast foreign policy establishment, whose members gathered regularly in the closed conference rooms of the Harold Pratt House.*

The most daunting problem of foreign policy in these years was the political significance of nuclear weaponry, by then in the arsenals of both the White House and the Kremlin. Destructive power unimaginable to earlier generations seemed to transform world politics and the nature of war as a continuation of policy by other means. On January 12, 1954, Secretary of State John Foster Dulles delivered a major public address to a Council dinner. (Following the precedent of the Clemenceau meeting in the Council's first year, the off-the-record status of deliberations was occasionally waived for distinguished speakers.) "There is no local defense which alone will contain the mighty land power of the communist world," Dulles declared. "Local defenses must be reinforced by the further deterrent of massive retaliatory power." The policy of the Eisenhower administration was to depend primarily "upon a great capacity to retaliate."

No special sensitivity to the language of diplomacy was necessary to comprehend the chilling import of these remarks. The Council convened a discussion group on Nuclear Weapons and Foreign Policy, in the year 1954–55. To chronicle the discussions, at the recommendation of Council members Arthur Schlesinger, Jr., McGeorge Bundy, and William Yandell Elliott (covering the range from liberal to hard-line, in public perception) the Council tapped a young scholar named Henry A. Kissinger. Taking leave from the Harvard faculty, Kissinger spent the academic year 1955–56 working at the Harold Pratt House. Reflecting upon the discussions of the group, and guiding them toward conclusions he had reached in his own research, Kissinger published in 1957 the book that earned him a national reputation, *Nuclear Weapons and Foreign Policy*. To the bemusement of his colleagues on 68th Street, the book reached the list of national best-sellers, hardly expected of a publication of the Council on Foreign Relations.

Kissinger went on to publish 12 articles in *Foreign Affairs* before he entered government as President Nixon's national security adviser in 1969. And over two decades, the Council's study and discussion groups served as

---

* One of the most visible targets of the red-baiters, the controversial Alger Hiss, was quietly dropped from Council membership, for successive years' nonpayment of annual dues. John Temple Swing, executive vice president of the Council until 1993, enjoyed informing new members over the years that the only other prominent figure dropped from the rolls for failing to pay dues was Richard Nixon.

Council members Zbigniew Brzezinski and Henry A. Kissinger at the Harold Pratt House in 1965, the year the Council published Brzezinski's *Alternative to Partition.* Eight years earlier Kissinger made his mark with the publication of *Nuclear Weapons and Foreign Policy.*

an important breeding ground for the doctrines of strategic stability, mutual deterrence, arms control, and nuclear nonproliferation that guided American foreign policy for the years of the Cold War.

The Council turned in earnest to the problem of communist China early in the 1960s. Various Council publications had started developing the idea of a "two-China" policy—recognition of both the Nationalist government of Taiwan and the communist government on the mainland. This, Council authors suggested, might be the least bad policy direction. Professor A. Doak Barnett published a trail-blazing book for the Council in 1960, *Communist China and Asia*. A major Council study of relations between the United States and China commenced in 1964, the year China exploded its first nuclear bomb; the group met systematically for the next four years. "Contentment with the present stalemate in relations with the Chinese is not statesmanship," declared Robert Blum of the Asia Society, the first director of the project. "American impatience and the strong currents of political emotion often make it impossible to plan ahead to manage our policy in a persevering but flexible way."

This seemed just the sort of political stalemate that the Council on Foreign Relations, free of electoral and partisan constraints, was endowed to repair. Midway through the project, the Council published an analysis of public opinion called *The American People and China* by A. T. Steele, who reached the unexpected conclusion that Americans were more willing than many of their elected officeholders to forge new relations with China. This study argued that it was only a steady diet of hostile public statements that had made Americans "disposed to believe the worst of communist China and they [the Chinese] the worst of us." In 1969 the Council summed up the project under the title, *The United States and China in World Affairs*, publication came just as Richard Nixon, a longtime and outspoken foe of Chinese communism, became president of the United States. (Some months earlier, Nixon himself had chosen *Foreign Affairs* as his forum for exploring a fresh look at Asia in general, and China in particular.) Tilting at the long-prevailing freeze, the Council's project defined a two-China policy with careful analysis. It advocated acquiescence in mainland Chinese membership in the United Nations, and argued that America must "abandon its effort to maintain the fiction that the Nationalist regime is the government of China."

Kissinger, acting as Nixon's national security adviser, embarked on a secret mission to Beijing in 1971, to make official, exploratory contact with the communist regime.* Nixon himself followed in 1972. The delicate process of

---

* Accompanying Kissinger on this momentous flight was his personal aide, Winston Lord, a former Foreign Service officer. Lord, who became president of the Council on Foreign Relations in 1977, possessed a flair for the dramatic under a pose of caution. At the crucial moment in the secret diplomatic flight to Beijing, the young aide strolled to the forward compartment of Kissinger's aircraft and casually waited there until he was sure they had passed over the ground frontier; with delight undiminished over years to come, Lord proclaimed that he was thus the first American official to cross into communist China.

Allen Dulles (right) welcomes to the Pratt House Indian Prime
Minister Jawaharlal Nehru and his sister Vijaylaxmi Pandit, Indian
ambassador to the United Nations and first female president of the
General Assembly.

normalizing diplomatic relations between the United States and China was
completed in 1978 by Kissinger's successor as secretary of state, Cyrus R.
Vance, a leading Council officer before and after his government service.

CONSENSUS ENDANGERED

NO ONE WHO KNEW of the Inquiry or the proto-Council on Foreign
Relations would have recognized their successor organization by the 1960s.
The elite dinner club of Wall Street bankers and their academic protégés
had grown into a broader-based community of Americans with expertise
and responsibility for the United States' role in world affairs.

Beyond the diplomatic reference works and *Foreign Affairs*, which had established the Council's presence in the foreign-policy community, came a flow of analytical books, many of which confirmed their authors onto career paths toward high government responsibility. The Council published Zbigniew Brzezinski's *Alternative to Partition*, an analysis of Europe divided between East and West, in 1965; a decade later he became the national security adviser to President Jimmy Carter. Studies of world economic relations had long been a mainstay of the Council's program, under the dedicated guidance of Senior Fellow William Diebold, Jr., even though economic policy was unfamiliar terrain to the typical diplomat of the era. Richard N. Cooper's *The Economics of Interdependence*, published in 1968, attracted wide attention; Cooper became the top economic officer of the State Department in the Carter administration. That same year, Professor Stanley Hoffmann of Harvard was introduced to a broader community of readers with his major study, *Gulliver's Troubles: The Setting of American Foreign Policy*.

In 1962 the Council had initiated a program to bring selected Air Force officers, on their way to flag rank, to the Harold Pratt House for a year of research and reflection with their civilian counterparts. This became a pilot project, with no intent at pun, and succeeded to the extent that the Army, Navy, and, eventually, Marine Corps asked for and received similar access.

In 1967 the Rockefeller Brothers Fund invited the Council to devise a fellowship program for promising scholars aged 27 to 35 from university faculties and the civil service. Some among the older Council directors expressed concern that a corps of younger fellows might distract the institution from its primary attentions to the established membership, average age close to 60. But the board authorized John Temple Swing of the Council staff to manage the experimental fellowship program, essentially on his own time. The result was the Council's International Affairs Fellowship Program, which continues three decades later to encourage younger scholars to supplement their academic work with practical experience in government, and government officials to take a year away from their job pressures to reflect and write on their experiences in office.

Over the coming decades, with each year's Military Fellows and civilian International Affairs Fellows, plus visitors from the expanding Committees across the country, the corridors of the Harold Pratt House awoke to curiosity and youth, to stimulate the thought habits of the mature members.

"Whatever it is, it isn't paper."

Inevitably, a vague unease arose about another group of competent Americans who had long and unhesitatingly been excluded from the Council. Alger Hiss, of all people, had first voiced the sentiment, back in the late 1940s, "that at least one woman" should serve on a public committee growing out of the Council.[7] Actual Council membership for women (ladies, as they were then called) still seemed beyond contemplation. A few intrepid members persisted in raising the delicate matter, leading one Council veteran to complain, "If you let one woman in, how can we keep our wives out?" Even more ominous, according to a worldly member of the staff, gentlemen members seemed worried about how they could comfortably explain their attendance at dinner meetings, running well into the evening, when unattached ladies were also present. The issue festered, unresolved, until the end of the 1960s.

Choosing members from another underrepresented group, the leaders of organized labor, also continued to frustrate the notables of the Council in their halting efforts to enlarge their community. At the end of World War II, there had been two: David Dubinsky and Robert J. Watt of the American

'YOU CONGRESS TYPES ARE SO DAMN SMART WITH THIS FOREIGN POLICY STUFF—HELP HENRY TURN THE LADDER!'

Federation of Labor. In May 1946 the directors voted to invite more representatives of the labor movement into the membership. Carefully chosen invitations went out; only two more accepted. Their numbers grew over the coming decades, and two presidents of the AFL-CIO, Lane Kirkland and Thomas R. Donahue, along with Glenn Watts, president of the Communications Workers of America, served terms on the Council's board of directors.

The most fruitful ground for new members turned out to be the so-called "in-and-outers"—businessmen, lawyers, and academics described by social scientists like C. Wright Mills as an influential "power elite." Two widely quoted critics of the Council, Laurence H. Shoup and William Minter, studied the *curriculum vitae* of 502 government officials in high positions from 1945 to 1972, and found that more than half of them were members of the Council on Foreign Relations.* Richard Barnet, a scholar elected to Council membership in 1969 who remained a frequent critic,

---

* High officials, in this study, ranged from the presidents of the United States to assistant secretaries in the State, War, Navy, and Defense Departments, undersecretaries at Treasury and Commerce; the Joint Chiefs of Staff, White House assistants, ambassadors to (only) France, Germany, Britain, and the U.S.S.R., and heads of agencies such as the Marshall Plan administration and the Export-Import Bank.

noted that membership in the Council on Foreign Relations could well be considered "a rite of passage for an aspiring national security manager."

In the days of the Inquiry, and in the decade following, the elite engaged in shaping American foreign policy could count on an internal consensus; disputes of substance and style marred the margins, of course, but a core of civility and mutual respect permitted the airing of differences within shared assumptions. Even in the late 1930s, when a schism over international responsibility threatened the body politic, the Council could accommodate the differences within its own collegial environment. Intervention versus isolation in the looming war against fascism was heatedly argued in Council meetings, inspiring countless speeches, articles, and at least one major book arguing for intervention. Then the dinner plates were lifted, the cigars passed around, and the fellowship restored.

The same cannot be said about the national dilemma that hit the United States in the 1960s. On the war in Vietnam, not a single Council study group was convened between 1964 and 1968, crucial years when American military support for the government of President Diem turned, under his successors, into an American land war on the continent of Asia. Across the nation and within the Harold Pratt House, passions were too high and divisions too deep to permit extensive presentation of diverging views in the civilized encounters that had previously characterized the Council. Perhaps it was the inevitable effect of an expanding, more heterogeneous membership; clearly the mood of shared underlying manners that had permitted a gentlemanly airing of differences in the 1930s no longer prevailed in the 1960s.

Typically, it was *Foreign Affairs* that broke the anguished reticence that had immobilized the rest of the Council. In 1968, after the disastrous Tet offensive and amid talk of starting truce negotiations, Armstrong opened large sections of three successive issues of his journal to the topic of Vietnam. He invited Kissinger, then still at Harvard, to contribute an article outlining how a settlement might be reached; the article appeared in January 1969, just as Kissinger became President Nixon's national security adviser. Armstrong minced no words about his own position, eloquently critical of the war policies that tore apart both nations, Vietnam and the United States. Americans had "failed to understand the people and society we were setting out to help," the editor wrote in April 1968, and he warned against ignoring "how much the Vietnam war is isolating us from other nations."

But it was also *Foreign Affairs* that provoked open insurrection within

[49]

William P. Bundy was offered the *Foreign Affairs* editorship by Council Chairman David Rockefeller. Although the nomination initially led to some opposition within the membership over Bundy's involvement in Vietnam policymaking, he assumed the post in 1972 and had left a lasting mark by the time he retired in 1984. He is pictured (left) at a 1979 Pratt House function next to Arthur Schlesinger, Jr., Council member and former special assistant to President Kennedy, and Stanley Hoffmann (second from right).

the membership. In 1970, Hamilton Fish Armstrong announced his intention to retire after 45 formidable years at the helm of the Council's august journal. The new chairman, David Rockefeller, approached a family friend, William P. Bundy, as the two men met at the Harvard president's house before the Harvard-Yale football game, and offered him the post. Anti-war dissidents within the membership promptly rose in protest that someone with Bundy's record—a high CIA, Defense, and State Department official through the prosecution of the war—would be entrusted with an independent foreign policy journal. Hastily called meetings at the Harold Pratt

'May I have your autograph, please . . . '

House revealed unprecedented anger; members branded Bundy a "war criminal"; his defenders branded the protesters as "left-McCarthyites."*

Late in 1971, the studies committee of the board of directors concluded that the Council's program could no longer ignore the Vietnam war. This time, unlike the earlier projects of George Franklin and Henry Kissinger, no single author could be expected to convey radically divergent analyses. The Council decided to invite a series of essays to examine both the war policy and the effects that policy was provoking across American society. Clearly, this was an inquiry more ambitious and challenging than any the Council had tried before, and more than a year passed before the Studies Program could agree on a director for the project. They finally chose a former Foreign Service officer named W. Anthony Lake, who had served in

---

* One critic who argued that Bundy could not be objective about Vietnam policy was Professor Richard H. Ullman of Princeton. Three years later, Ullman joined the Council staff as director of studies. His first day on the job, he recalls, Bundy walked into his office extending a welcoming hand and expressing his determination to prove the professor wrong in doubting that he had the capacity for independent judgment required of *Foreign Affairs*. Over the coming years, Ullman freely acknowledged his earlier error, and his opinion that Bundy turned out to be a first-class editor.

In 1976, under the direction of former Foreign Service officer W. Anthony Lake (shown here on the left in 1994 with Robert S. McNamara, former secretary of defense), the Council issued its first comprehensive analysis of the war in Southeast Asia. "Even if we do not want to think about the war, it has changed us. . . . We are condemned to act out the unconscious, as well as conscious, 'lessons' we have learned," wrote Lake in *The Vietnam Legacy*. He became national security adviser to President Clinton in 1992.

Vietnam, returned to join Kissinger's staff at the White House, and then abruptly resigned in protest in 1970.

"Even if we do not want to think about the war, it has changed us," Lake wrote. "We are condemned to act out the unconscious, as well as con-scious, 'lessons' we have learned." To present widely divergent perspectives, he commissioned 22 distinguished American and foreign authors, ranging from Irving Kristol to Earl C. Ravenal, Maxwell Taylor to Paul C. Warnke, Richard C. Holbrooke, Leslie H. Gelb, Morton H. Halperin, and Senators John G. Tower and Hubert Humphrey. Concluding his introduction to the anthology as the Vietnam war came to its dismal denouement, Lake wrote:

'...AND I THINK IT WOULD BE NICE IF WE COULD NUKE IRAN OR FREE POLAND SOMETIME IN OCTOBER...'

The Vietnam experience may have so damaged American confidence that it intensifies what could be a nationalistic reaction to problems that can only be solved through international action. The dangerous irony is that the global crisis in food, energy, and population could itself push Americans in a nationalistic direction, as it comes more and more to intrude into our everyday lives. The United States is discovering, after decades of what seemed like relative immunity from the economic and social consequences of events abroad, that it is just another nation—tremendously powerful, but almost as vulnerable to others as they have been to us.

The Vietnam Legacy, published in 1976, was the first comprehensive analysis of the war in Vietnam to issue from the Council on Foreign Relations. Anthony Lake eventually became national security adviser to President Bill Clinton.

THE SECOND TRANSFORMATION

"PERHAPS 50 YEARS is all a select organization can last, especially in these permissive years," mourned the Council's Walter Mallory in retire-

Susan E. Rice, Charlayne Hunter-Gault, and Sharon Wilkinson (from left facing camera) at the 1996 Diversity Program Conference, "Defining the National Interest: Minorities and U.S. Foreign Policy in the 21st Century."

ment, at the height of membership unrest over Vietnam. A quarter-century has passed since Mallory's lament, and the Council has more than lasted. It remains a select organization, to be sure, but one that has responded to the changing face of American society and the demands of international responsibility upon that society.

The Council on Foreign Relations is no longer unique in its purpose. A dozen or more research institutions around the world attempt to analyze the changing global scene without partisan bias, but with a clear focus on the policy implications for their respective governments. They publish rich and admirable journals that expand the understanding of their populace, just as the lonely voice of *Foreign Affairs* set out to do 75 years ago. Study and discussion groups among experts and concerned citizens, which the

David Rockefeller and Prime Minister of Israel Golda Meir at a 1973 black tie function at the Harold Pratt House.

Council pioneered in the 1920s, are now commonplace—in university research institutes, on television and the Internet, forums that the founders could not have begun to contemplate in their dedication to spreading public understanding of complex matters of diplomacy.

Early in the 1970s, *Foreign Affairs* made a modest one-word change in its mission statement. From the founding, the journal had set out, among its purposes, to "guide" American public opinion. The verb was changed; the purpose became to "inform" public opinion. Public interest in international relations is no longer in need of guidance or stimulation, as Elihu Root argued it was in 1922. The typical American no longer needs to be told that developments across the globe reflect upon his or her daily life. But the busy public does seek and need information that is reliable and unvarnished.

There sometimes lurks among experts in high office a sense that they need not respect the opinions of those lacking access to the detailed information available within the "classified" preserves of government. The Council has never offered itself as a repository of classified diplomatic or military files. But those on bureaucratic staffs who base their actions on information that cannot be shared (in some form) with the public have

David Rockefeller escorts Egyptian President Anwar al-Sadat (left) through the doorway of the Harold Pratt House in 1981, the year of the latter's assassination.

learned over the years that they do so only at the peril of their policy goals. Discussions at the Harold Pratt House remain confidential—not because they deal with secret information, but largely because members and invited guests often use the occasions to test tentative opinions they have not yet fully thought through and developed.

The turn of the 1970s brought a fundamental renovation of the Council's leadership. David Rockefeller, head of the Chase Manhattan Bank and an active Council member for 30 years, became chairman of the board in 1970, succeeding John J. McCloy, who had served for 17 years. Leadership of *Foreign Affairs* passed from Armstrong to Bundy, and the board decided to

'O beautiful for spacious skies
For amber waves of grain . . . '

seek out a full-time chief executive officer. Working closely with Rockefeller in modernizing the Council's management was Cyrus R. Vance,
retired from service in the Defense Department to resume his New York
law practice. "There comes a time in the life of every institution when
things just need to be shaken up," Vance explained many years later, "and
that is what we set out to do."

As the first president, Rockefeller and Vance chose Bayless Manning, a
Council member since 1961 who had recently lived on the West Coast as
dean of the Stanford Law School. Just before Manning's arrival, the board
finally resolved the issue of admitting women as members; by 1971, 18
women had been invited to join. At the same time, the directors created a
category of term members, those aged between 21 and 27 who showed
promise in the Council's purposes, for five-year terms, without commitment (as with the rest of Council members) to life-long participation. Nine
of the 48 members elected in 1971 were term members.

The median age of the 1,600 Council members in the early 1970s was 58.
By 1975, 28 percent of the membership had been elected within the past three
years, and through a conscious effort to enlarge and diversify, the trend
toward youth and variety of background gained momentum. The member-

David Rockefeller (left) and Bayless Manning in conversation at the Harold Pratt House. A Council member for 30 years, Rockefeller assumed the chairmanship in 1970. He and Cyrus R. Vance created the new post of full-time president, a position first filled by Manning in 1971.

Israeli Foreign Minister Shimon Peres and Council member Rita Hauser at a 1994 study group session.

King Hussein Bin Talal and Queen Noor of Jordan (shown here on the left) are received by former *Washington Post* publisher and Council member Katharine Graham (far right) and Director of the Council's Middle East Forum Judith Kipper.

ship rolls doubled over the next 20 years. In terms of occupation, members from business and banking dropped modestly as a fraction of the whole (from 28 to 25 percent), as academic members, foundation executives, officers in the not-for-profit sector, and media representatives increased their numbers. The average age of newly elected members now tends to be about 47, fully 10 years younger than the membership as a whole.

In 1972, the new Council leadership took another controversial step: it opened an office in Washington to supplement the established membership and research facilities in New York. This modest outpost, as it was considered when it began, has burgeoned into a full program of meetings and fellows for the growing number of Washington-based members, including representatives from both the executive and legislative branches of government. By the mid-1990s, more than two-thirds of Council members lived

While approaching Chinese airspace during Secretary of State Kissinger's 1971 secret mission to the People's Republic of China, Winston Lord (on the left) moved to the front of the plane in order to be the first American diplomat to enter communist China. He was later President Reagan's ambassador to the PRC. Serving as Council president from 1977 to 1985, Lord was succeeded by President Pro-tempore John Temple Swing. The two converse over drinks in 1983.

and worked beyond a 50-mile radius of New York; Washington and Boston retain the largest share, but a significant increase in membership has taken place on the West Coast, in the Midwest, and in such southern cities as Dallas and Atlanta.

Geographical dispersion of the Council's membership seemed a natural response to the evolution of American society as a whole. Interest and expertise in international affairs is no longer clustered in two or three large eastern cities, as it was when the Council was young. But this dispersion presents obvious logistical and financial problems for an institution dedicated to the convening of knowledgeable professionals for continuous personal contact. Winston Lord, who succeeded Manning as the Council's president in 1977, launched a major effort at long-term national outreach through regional membership meetings and ever more frequent travel by Council officers and fellows. Lord's successor, Peter Tarnoff, continued these experiments during the 1980s and promoted the novel departure of opening occasional Council meetings to public television coverage. Leslie

Peter Tarnoff (right, shown here with Oscar Arias Sánchez, Nobel Peace Prize Laureate and former Costa Rican president) succeeded Lord as Council president in 1986 and instituted a number of innovations, including the opening of certain Council events to public television coverage. Tarnoff and Lord went on to serve in Warren Christopher's State Department as undersecretary for political affairs and assistant secretary for East Asian and Pacific affairs respectively.

H. Gelb, who became the Council's president in 1993, carried these activities further by establishing regular programs for members throughout the country and staging hearings and debates for television.

The substance of the Council's program was transformed in parallel with its membership and operating style. Starting early in the 1970s, Richard H. Ullman, the director of studies, and Manning designed a major research effort, to be called the 1980s Project, to define the new issues and policy responses of an international society evolving beyond the East-West conflict. Unlike its predecessors, the Inquiry and the War and Peace Studies, the 1980s Project opted for full participation by members and non-members alike, and planned for publication of its research to stimulate a broad professional audience, not just those with government responsibility.

Between 1977 and 1982, the Council published nearly two dozen policy-oriented books that collectively served to define what became known as "global issues," many of them unfamiliar to conventional diplomatic thinking. With the Cold War still the fundamental fact of international life, study groups produced monographs on the military balance, regional conflicts, and arms control, both nuclear and conventional. But fully one-third of the Council's papers dealt with economic and other issues that earlier diplomatic generations had considered beneath notice. The variety of titles

AUTH

Detente

revealed the broadened agenda of foreign policy: *Beyond the North-South Stalemate, International Disaster Relief, Enhancing Global Human Rights, Controlling the Future Arms Trade.*

"The product was anything but splashy," wrote Leonard Silk, economics columnist of *The New York Times* and an active Council member. "Prose tended toward the dull and academic; conclusions toward the inconclusive." As it turned out, the title of the project was a little premature; not until the 1990s did the issues explored truly dominate the international agenda. But many 1980s Project authors were by then installed in government policy-making positions, and when the Cold War came to its unexpectedly sudden end the Council had provided for the public record an impressive database for the global issues confronting coming generations.[8]

David Rockefeller stepped down as the Council's active chairman in 1985 to be succeeded by Peter G. Peterson, an investment banker and former secretary of commerce, who had brought creative management to the Council's soaring endowment and an appreciation for its longstanding intellectual stimulus to businessmen and scholars alike. Lord and Tarnoff, both having been career Foreign Service officers, moved from the Council presidency into senior government offices—Lord to become ambassador to China and then assistant secretary of state for East Asian and Pacific affairs,

Among the Council's directors, Chairman of the
Board Peter G. Peterson (above center, flanked by
former Secretaries of State Cyrus R. Vance and
Henry A. Kissinger), Vice Chairman of the Board
Maurice R. Greenberg (shown at right), and
Jeane J. Kirkpatrick (shown below at left with
Council President Leslie H. Gelb and Senior
Vice President and National Director Alton Frye
at a Washington, D.C., Council meeting) "per-
petuated the nonpartisan leadership that had gov-
erned the Council since the years of Elihu Root
and Hamilton Fish Armstrong."

Rigoberta Menchú Tum (right), the Guatemalan Nobel Peace Prize Laureate and a member of the International Advisory Board, with Council Board member Mario L. Baeza at a 1994 meeting, "The Peace Process and the Mayan Communities in Guatemala and Chiapas."

Tarnoff to be President Clinton's undersecretary of state for political affairs. Council members continued the "in-and-out" progression, established by the previous generations, through changing American administrations.

The sudden end of the Cold War at the turn of the 1990s brought the Council on Foreign Relations, in common with foreign-policy thinkers the world over, to a dramatic juncture of regrouping and redefinition. The sense of purpose stimulated by the X article of 1947 was, virtually at a stroke, annulled. But the Council, after all, had carved out a leading role in international affairs for a quarter-century before the Cold War. Thanks to the 1980s Project, its members and fellows were not unprepared for the intellectual demands of the post–Cold War era. In 1990, the Council published an important survey entitled *Sea Changes: American Foreign Policy in a World Transformed,* in which 17 influential experts showed how global relations were not merely in transition but on the brink of fundamental transformation.

Among the directors, Peterson, Jeane J. Kirkpatrick, and Maurice R. Greenberg perpetuated the nonpartisan leadership that had governed the

Along with former *Foreign Affairs* editor William G. Hyland, Lenin's last heir inspects a copy of the Council's journal annotated by the founder of Bolshevism. Gorbachev has yet to contribute his own annotated copy of *Foreign Affairs* to the Council archives.

Council since the years of Elihu Root and Hamilton Fish Armstrong. At *Foreign Affairs,* Bundy's successor, William G. Hyland, passed the editorship to James F. Hoge, Jr., in 1992, who, in the Armstrong tradition, came in as a journalist rather than an officer of government. Under Hoge's guidance, the flagship journal expanded its scope of coverage and offered a new variety of content without sacrificing the authority that its major articles had long conveyed. The professional background of the new president, Leslie H. Gelb, bridged the old divides; Gelb had been a scholar and one of the 1980s Project authors, a Pentagon and State Department official, and then a correspondent and columnist for *The New York Times.*

Under Gelb's leadership, the Council has focused its efforts on nurturing the next generation of foreign policy leaders, expanding the Council's outreach through national programs and the regular use of television for hearings and debates on major policy issues, and enlarging the Studies Program

[65]

James F. Hoge, Jr. (left) assumed the editorship of *Foreign Affairs* in 1992 upon William G. Hyland's retirement. The two pose in that year with Council Director Theodore C. Sorensen (right).

division with two stated purposes: figuring out the rules and rhythms of foreign policy and developing new ideas for America and the international community.

"Even the best and most open of minds reared in times as searing as the past 50 years cannot be rewired to today's startlingly different world," Gelb wrote in the annual report as the Council turned 75. Building for the 21st century, the Council is pursuing a conscious campaign, extending the effort begun in the 1970s, to locate and engage the new thinkers of the next generation. "We believe that they will have special insights into our new world," Gelb argues. "They have grown up with computers, worked hand-in-hand with Russians and others on joint business ventures, and run non-government organizations more powerful than many governments. Our challenge is to bring them together regularly, to address the future."

Novel techniques for defining and disseminating ideas nurtured at the

Harold Pratt House have been developed to supplement the traditional study and discussion groups: the Council started sending high-level groups of directors and members to meet with foreign leaders in Russia, China, Hungary, Poland, Vietnam, and the Middle East. The Council's board of directors now meets regularly with an International Advisory Board, composed of leading figures in business, government, and scholarship overseas, to help define issues for attention and add international perspective to the evolving Council program. Though most of the Council meetings continue in the tradition of confidential exchanges, critical public issues and distinguished speakers, like Clemenceau long before, are presented before a wide audience sometimes through national television, in the form of debates between speakers of opposing viewpoints.

This momentum springs from a firm grounding in a long and illustrious history. Mikhail Gorbachev, the last head of the Soviet Union, visited the Harold Pratt House in 1992. The heir to the twentieth century's Bolshevism paused over a display of the opened copy of *Foreign Affairs'* first 1922 issue with Lenin's and Radek's penciled annotations. Gorbachev remarked that he, too, had made some marginal notes in an issue of the Council's journal that had been translated for him. (Gorbachev has not yet offered to contribute that annotated copy for the Council's archives.) From the Inquiry to the incubator of ideas, the Council on Foreign Relations is continuing to test itself—in growth, adaptation, and respect for a unique heritage.

AUTHOR'S NOTE

WILLIAM DIEBOLD, JR., a mainstay of the Council on Foreign Relations for nearly four decades, defined the output of the Studies Program in succinct fashion: "Policy conclusions reached by an individual after hearing discussion and having his [or her] ideas criticized by a group—but not negotiated for agreement or consensus." This was the working methodology devised in the Council's early years and it continues to the present day. It is on this formula that the present seventy-fifth anniversary history was prepared.

When the officers and directors of the Council invited me to take on the project, we all agreed that the work would be the responsibility of a single author, not a committee. Informed, it is not necessarily authoritative. This is an "authorized" history only in the sense that the Council is publishing it; the history of these 75 years is so rich and varied that another author, bringing a different set of idiosyncrasies to the project, might have written about the Council quite differently. As the designated author, I was given no ground rules, no instructions on what to include or omit, and no one of the board, staff, or membership asserted any claim to "approve" what I would write.

In keeping with the time-tested practice, however, I shared working drafts with a few individuals who could react with special knowledge; many of them I had come to know as friends and colleagues during my two decades in the Council. An encouraging number of them came back with many pages of comments, general and specific, to inform and enrich the final writing—just the process that guides any Council publication by a single author. I deeply value the interest they showed and their generosity in sharing their various insights. Responsibility for judgments of fact, emphasis, and context, nonetheless, is mine alone.

To the following colleagues who gave me their comments on the manuscript's early versions I express sincere gratitude: Bill Bundy, John Campbell, Bill Diebold, Patricia Dorff, Alton Frye, Les Gelb, Judith Gustafson, David Kellogg, Daniel Kohns, Elise Lewis, Bayless Manning, Jan Murray, Pete Peterson, David Rockefeller, Ted Sorensen, John Swing, Peter Tarnoff, Dick Ullman, and Alice Victor.

[68]

APPENDIX

Historical Roster of Directors and Officers

Directors

Isaiah Bowman	1921–50	John H. Williams	1937–64
Archibald Cary Coolidge	1921–28	Lewis W. Douglas	1940–64
Paul D. Cravath	1921–40	Edward Warner	1940–49
John W. Davis	1921–55	Clarence E. Hunter	1942–53
Norman H. Davis	1921–44	Myron C. Taylor	1943–59
Stephen P. Duggan	1921–50	Henry M. Wriston	1943–67
John H. Finley	1921–29	Thomas K. Finletter	1944–67
Edwin F. Gay	1921–45	William A. M. Burden	1945–74
David F. Houston	1921–27	Walter H. Mallory	1945–68
Otto H. Kahn	1921–34	Philip D. Reed	1945–69
Frank L. Polk	1921–43	Winfield W. Riefler	1945–50
Whitney H. Shepardson	1921–66	David Rockefeller	1949–85
William R. Shepherd	1921–27	W. Averell Harriman	1950–55
Paul M. Warburg	1921–32	Joseph E. Johnson	1950–74
George M. Wickersham	1921–36	Grayson Kirk	1950–73
Allen W. Dulles	1927–69	Devereux C. Josephs	1951–58
Russell C. Leffingwell	1927–60	Elliott V. Bell	1953–66
George O. May	1927–53	John J. McCloy	1953–72
Wesley C. Mitchell	1927–34	Arthur H. Dean	1955–72
Owen D. Young	1927–40	Charles M. Spofford	1955–72
Hamilton Fish Armstrong	1928–72	Adlai E. Stevenson	1958–62
Charles P. Howland	1929–31	William C. Foster	1959–72
Walter Lippmann	1932–37	Caryl P. Haskins	1961–75
Clarence M. Woolley	1932–35	James A. Perkins	1963–79
Frank Altschul	1934–72	William P. Bundy	1964–74
Philip C. Jessup	1934–42	Gabriel Hauge	1964–81
Harold W. Dodds	1935–43	Carroll L. Wilson	1964–79
Leon Fraser	1936–45	Douglas Dillon	1965–78
		Henry R. Labouisse	1965–74

Robert V. Roosa	1966–81
Lucian W. Pye	1966–82
Alfred C. Neal	1967–76
Bill Moyers	1967–74
Cyrus R. Vance	1968–76, 1981–87
Hedley Donovan	1969–79
Najeeb E. Halaby	1970–72
Bayless Manning	1971–77
W. Michael Blumenthal	1972–77, 1979–84
Zbigniew Brzezinski	1972–77
Elizabeth Drew	1972–77
George S. Franklin	1972–83
Marshall D. Shulman	1972–77
Martha Redfield Wallace	1972–82
Paul C. Warnke	1972–77
Peter G. Peterson	1973–83, 1984–
Robert O. Anderson	1974–80
Edward K. Hamilton	1974–83
Harry C. McPherson, Jr.	1974–77
Elliot L. Richardson	1974–75
Franklin Hall Williams	1975–83
Nicholas deB. Katzenbach	1975–86
Paul A. Volcker	1975–79, 1988–
Theodore M. Hesburgh	1976–85
Lane Kirkland	1976–86
George H. W. Bush	1977–79
Lloyd N. Cutler	1977–79
Philip L. Geyelin	1977–87
Henry A. Kissinger	1977–81
Winston Lord	1977–85
Stephen Stamas	1977–89
Marina v.N. Whitman	1977–87
C. Peter McColough	1978–87

Richard L. Gelb	1979–88
Graham T. Allison, Jr.	1979–88
William D. Ruckelshaus	1979–83
James F. Hoge, Jr.	1980–84
George P. Shultz	1980–82
William D. Rogers	1980–90
Walter B. Wriston	1981–87
Lewis T. Preston	1981–88
Warren Christopher	1982–91
Alan Greenspan	1982–88
Robert A. Scalapino	1982–89
Harold Brown	1983–92
Stanley Hoffmann	1983–92
Juanita M. Kreps	1983–89
Brent Scowcroft	1983–89
Clifton R. Wharton, Jr.	1983–92
Donald F. McHenry	1984–93
B. R. Inman	1985–93
Jeane J. Kirkpatrick	1985–94
Peter Tarnoff	1986–93
Charles McC. Mathias, Jr.	1986–92
Ruben F. Mettler	1986–92
James E. Burke	1987–95
Richard B. Cheney	1987–89, 1993–95
Robert F. Erburu	1987–
Karen Elliott House	1987–
Glenn E. Watts	1987–90
Thomas S. Foley	1988–94
James D. Robinson III	1988–91
Strobe Talbott	1988–93
John L. Clendenin	1989–94
William S. Cohen	1989–
Joshua Lederberg	1989–
John S. Reed	1989–92
Alice M. Rivlin	1989–92
William J. Crowe, Jr.	1990–93

Thomas R. Donahue	1990–	*Chairmen of the Board*	
Richard C. Holbrooke	1991–93	Russell C. Leffingwell	1946–53
	1996–	John J. McCloy	1953–70
Robert D. Hormats	1991–	David Rockefeller	1970–85
John E. Bryson	1992–	Peter G. Peterson	1985–
Maurice R. Greenberg	1992–	*Vice Chairmen of the Board*	
Karen N. Horn	1992–95	Grayson Kirk	1971–73
James R. Houghton	1992–96	Cyrus R. Vance	1973–76,
Charlayne Hunter-Gault	1992–		1985–87
Kenneth W. Dam	1992–	Douglas Dillon	1976–78
Donna E. Shalala	1992–93	Carroll L. Wilson	1978–79
Alton Frye	1993	Warren Christopher	1987–91
Richard N. Cooper	1993–94	Harold Brown	1991–92
Rita E. Hauser	1993–	B. R. Inman	1992–93
E. Gerald Corrigan	1993–95	Jeane J. Kirkpatrick	1993–94
Leslie H. Gelb	1993–	Maurice R. Greenberg	1994–
Paul A. Allaire	1993–	*Presidents*	
Robert E. Allen	1993–		
Theodore C. Sorensen	1993–	John W. Davis	1921–33
Garrick Utley	1993–	George W. Wickersham	1933–36
Carla A. Hills	1994–	Norman H. Davis	1936–44
Helene L. Kaplan	1994–96	Russell C. Leffingwell	1944–46
Frank G. Zarb	1994–96	Allen W. Dulles	1946–50
Robert B. Zoellick	1994–	Henry M. Wriston	1951–64
Les Aspin	1995	Grayson Kirk	1964–71
Mario L. Baeza	1995–	Bayless Manning	1971–77
Peggy Dulany	1995–	Winston Lord	1977–85
Jessica P. Einhorn	1995–	John Temple Swing*	1985–86
William J. McDonough	1995–	Peter Tarnoff	1986–93
Frank Savage	1995–	Alton Frye	1993
George Soros	1995–	Leslie H. Gelb	1993–
Hannah Holborn Gray	1995–	*Honorary President*	
George J. Mitchell	1995–	Elihu Root	1931–37
Louis V. Gerstner, Jr.	1995–	*Executive Vice President*	
Lee Cullum	1996–	John Temple Swing	1986–93

* Pro-tempore

Vice Presidents

Paul D. Cravath	1921–33
Norman H. Davis	1933–36
Edwin F. Gay	1933–40
Frank L. Polk	1940–43
Russell C. Leffingwell	1943–44
Allen W. Dulles	1944–46
Isaiah Bowman	1945–49
Henry M. Wriston	1950–51
David Rockefeller	1950–70
Frank Altschul	1951–71
Devereux C. Josephs	1951–52
David W. MacEachron	1972–74
John Temple Swing	1972–86
Alton Frye	1987–93
William H. Gleysteen, Jr.	1987–89
John A. Millington	1987–
Margaret Osmer-McQuade	1987–93
Nicholas X. Rizopoulos	1989–94
Karen M. Sughrue	1993–
Abraham F. Lowenthal	1995–
Janice L. Murray	1995–
David J. Vidal	1995–
Ethan B. Kapstein	1995–96

Senior Vice Presidents

Alton Frye	1993–
Kenneth H. Keller	1993–95
Larry L. Fabian	1994–95
Michael P. Peters	1995–

Secretaries

Edwin F. Gay	1921–33
Allen W. Dulles	1933–44
Frank Altschul	1944–72
John Temple Swing	1972–87
Judith Gustafson	1987–

Treasurers

Edwin F. Gay	1921–33
Whitney H. Shepardson	1933–42
Clarence E. Hunter	1942–51
Devereux C. Josephs	1951–52
Elliott V. Bell	1952–64
Gabriel Hauge	1964–81
Peter G. Peterson	1981–85
C. Peter McColough	1985–87
Lewis T. Preston	1987–88
James E. Burke	1988–89
David Woodbridge	1989–94
Janice L. Murray	1994–

Executive Directors

Hamilton Fish Armstrong	1922–28
Malcolm W. Davis	1925–27
Walter H. Mallory	1927–59
George S. Franklin, Jr.	1953–71

Directors of Studies

Percy W. Bidwell	1937–53
Philip E. Mosely	1955–63
Richard H. Ullman	1973–76
Abraham F. Lowenthal	1976–77
John C. Campbell	1977–78
Paul H. Kreisberg	1981–87
William H. Gleysteen, Jr.	1987–89
Nicholas X. Rizopoulos	1989–94
Kenneth H. Keller*	1994–95
Ethan B. Kapstein	1995–96
Kenneth Maxwell	1996–

Editors of Foreign Affairs

Archibald Cary Coolidge	1922–28
Hamilton Fish Armstrong	1928–72
William P. Bundy	1972–84
William G. Hyland	1984–92
James F. Hoge, Jr.	1992–

*Pro-tempore

NOTES

1. William P. Bundy, *The Council on Foreign Relations and Foreign Affairs: Notes for a History* (New York: Council on Foreign Relations, 1994), p. 22.
2. This statistical analysis is drawn from a study by Inderjeet Parmar, lecturer in American Studies at the University of Manchester (England), published in *The Journal of American Studies*, vol. 29, no. 1 (1995), pp. 73–95.
3. Michael Wala, *The Council on Foreign Relations and American Foreign Policy in the Early Cold War* (Providence: Berghahn Books, 1994), p. 62.
4. Wala, *The Council on Foreign Relations*, p. 76.
5. George Kennan, "Containment Then and Now," *Foreign Affairs*, vol. 65, no. 4 (Spring 1987), p. 890.
6. William Diebold, Jr., an influential economist on the Council staff, discussed the Eisenhower study group in a memorandum of September 4, 1990, now in the Council on Foreign Relations archives.
7. Wala, *The Council on Foreign Relations*, p. 195.
8. For an independent analysis of the 1980s Project, see Robert D. Schulzinger, *The Wise Men of Foreign Affairs* (New York: Columbia University Press, 1984), pp. 227–35.

FOR FURTHER READING

The Council on Foreign Relations has been blessed by two fine academic studies of its first half-century or so:

Robert D. Schulzinger, *The Wise Men of Foreign Affairs* (New York: Columbia University Press, 1984).
Michael Wala, *The Council on Foreign Relations and American Foreign Policy in the Early Cold War* (Providence: Berghahn Books, 1994).

Both authors made fair and comprehensive use of the Council archives that were available up to the point of their writing. This seventy-fifth anniversary history draws heavily upon their earlier researches.

The Council's own records of meetings, conferences, and study and discussion groups, a long row of bound books, is available for scholarly scrutiny at the Harold Pratt House, 58 East 68th Street, New York, NY 10021. These are supplemented by the papers of Hamilton Fish Armstrong and related *Foreign Affairs* files at the Seeley G. Mudd Manuscript Library at Princeton University. See also Armstrong's memoirs, *Peace and Counterpeace: From Wilson to Hitler* (New York: Harper & Row, 1971). A thoughtful analysis of the War and Peace Studies is: Carlo Maria Santoro, *Diffidence and Ambition: The Intellectual Sources of U.S. Foreign Policy* (Boulder: Westview Press, 1992; originally published in 1987 in Italian). The most important critical analysis of the Council is: Laurence H. Shoup and William Minter, *Imperial Brain Trust: The Council on Foreign Relations and United States Foreign Policy* (New York: Monthly Review Press, 1977).

A series of Council publications well conveys the organization's changing concerns. Informative annual reports have been published since the beginning and contain a wealth of institutional data. Other surveys include:

The Council on Foreign Relations: A Record of Fifteen Years, 1937.
The War and Peace Studies of the Council on Foreign Relations, 1946.
The Council on Foreign Relations: A Record of Twenty-five Years, 1947.

[74]

Whitney H. Shepardson, *Early History of the Council on Foreign Relations,* 1960.

Joseph Barber, *These Are the Committees,* 1964.

William P. Bundy, *The Council on Foreign Relations and Foreign Affairs: Notes for a History,* 1994.

Among the useful periodical depictions of the Council over the changing years are:

Joseph Kraft, "School for Statesmen," *Harper's,* July 1958.

Zygmunt Nagorski, "A Member of the CFR Talks Back," *National Review,* Dec. 9, 1977.

Elisabeth Jakab, "The Council on Foreign Relations," *Book Forum,* vol. 3, no. 4 (1978).

Inderjeet Parmar, "The Issue of State Power: The Council on Foreign Relations as a Case Study," *The Journal of American Studies,* vol. 29, no. 1 (1995).

INDEX

Communist China and Asia (Barnett), 43
Controlling the Future Arms Trade, 62
Coolidge, Archibald Cary, 17, 18
Cooper, Richard, 46
Costa Rica, 61
Curtis, Lionel, 12
Czechoslovakia, 13

Dallin, David, 31, 32
Dartmouth College, 38
Davis, John W., 7
Defense Department, 48n, 50, 57
"Defining the National Interest: Minorities and U.S. Foreign Policy in the 21st Century," 54
Democratic Party, 9, 13, 14, 29
Denmark, 25
Dickey, John Sloan, 38
Diebold, William, Jr., 46, 68
Dien Bien Phu, 40
Diversity Program Conference, 54
Dodds, Harold W., 27
Donahue, Thomas, 48
Dubinsky, David, 47
DuBois, W. E. B., 18
Dulles, Allen, 21–22, 32, 34, 38, 44; and the OSS, 26, 29; and the War and Peace Studies project, 24, 26
Dulles, John Foster, 9, 12–13, 22, 29, 32, 41
Dumbarton Oaks conference (1944), 25

Economics of Interdependence, The (Cooper), 46
Egypt, 56
Eisenhower, Dwight D., 39, 41
Elliott, William Yandell, 41
England. *See* Britain
Enhancing Global Human Rights, 62
European Community, 39

Fascism, 21–22
Ford Foundation, 29
Foreign Affairs, 26, 29, 54, 56, 64–65, 67; Armstrong as managing editor of, 18, 20–21; circulation of, growth in, 39; launch of, 12–14, 16–17; mission statement of, 55; Nixon's article in, 43; publication of the X Article in, 37–38; and the Vietnam War, 49
Foreign Affairs Bibliography, 29
Foreign Service, 62
France, 5, 10, 40
Franklin, George, 32, 34–35, 51
Frye, Alton, 63

Gelb, Leslie H., 52, 60–61, 63, 65–66
Germany, 1, 10, 20–21, 24, 26, 29, 35
Gleason, S. Everett, 30
Global issues, 61–62
Good Neighbor Policy, 19
Gorbachev, Mikhail, 65, 67
Graham, Katharine, 59
Great Britain, 5, 7–9, 21, 23
Greenberg, Maurice R., 63, 64
Greenland, 25
Gromyko, Andrei, 30–31, 32
Guatemala, 63
Gulliver's Troubles: The Setting of American Foreign Policy (Hoffmann), 46

Halperin, Morton H., 52
Hapsburg Empire, 13
Harold Pratt House, 29–30, 32, 35–36, 38, 41–42, 46, 49–51, 55–56, 58, 66–67
Harriman, W. Averell, 9, 10
Harvard University, 17–18, 27, 30, 38, 46, 49
Hauser, Rita, 58
Henderson, William, 40
Hiss, Alger, 29, 32, 41n, 47

ABOUT THE AUTHOR

PETER GROSE was managing editor and then executive editor of *Foreign Affairs* from 1984 to 1993. Previously he was the senior fellow for the Middle East at the Council on Foreign Relations; he has been a Council member since 1974.

He was a foreign and diplomatic correspondent for *The New York Times* starting in 1962, and was appointed to its editorial board in 1972. For the year 1977–78 he was deputy director of the Policy Planning Staff of the Department of State.

Born in Evanston, Illinois, Grose served as a U.S. Senate Page, graduated from Yale University in 1957, and received a Master's degree in Politics, Philosophy, and Economics from Oxford University. He is an Honorary Fellow of Oxford's Pembroke College.

Among his previous books are *Israel in the Mind of America* and, most recently, *Gentleman Spy: The Life of Allen Dulles.*

PHOTO AND CARTOON CREDITS

All pictures not credited below are from the Council on Foreign Relations archives.

1. Hall of Mirrors (National Archives), p. 4.
2. Georges Clemenceau (Museum of the City of New York), p. 11.
3. Dorothy Thompson (AP/Wide World Photos), p. 20.

Cartoons

1. "Council meeting." (Chris Weyant, 1996), pp. vi, vii.
2. "Looking a gift horse in the mouth." (Corbis-Bettmann), p. 3.
3. "And they are the leading members of the League of Nations . . ." (The Tribune, Chicago, 1920), p. 6.
4. "The only way we can save her." (The Tribune, Chicago, 1939), p. 22.
5. "It's the same thing without mechanical problems." (The Herblock Book, Beacon Press, 1952), p. 33.
6. "It's the Internationale . . ." (Drawing by Alan Dunn; © 1941, The New Yorker Magazine, Inc.), p. 34.
7. "In the name of peace, law and order—surrender." (Corbis-Bettmann), p. 45.
8. "Whatever it is, it isn't paper." (Mauldin. Reprinted with permission, Chicago Sun Times, © 1995), p. 47.
9. "You Congress types . . ." (United Press Syndicate, 1975), p. 48.
10. "May I have your autograph, please . . ." (United Press Syndicate, 1974), p. 51.
11. "And I think it would be nice . . ." (Universal Press Syndicate, 1980), p. 53.
12. "O beautiful for spacious skies . . ." (Universal Press Syndicate, 1975), p. 57.
13. "Detente." (Universal Press Syndicate, 1973), p. 62.